VIOLENCE IN OUR SCHOOLS, HOSPITALS AND PUBLIC PLACES

A PREVENTION AND MANAGEMENT GUIDE

VIOLENCE IN OUR SCHOOLS, HOSPITALS AND PUBLIC PLACES

A PREVENTION AND MANAGEMENT GUIDE

by

Eugene D. Wheeler & S. Anthony Baron, Ph.D.

Pathfinder Publishing of California

Ventura, CA 93003

VIOLENCE IN SCHOOLS, HOSPITALS AND PUBLIC PLACES

Published by:
Pathfinder Publishing of California
458 Dorothy Avenue
Ventura, CA 93003
(805) 642-9278

Copyright © 1994 by Eugene D. Wheeler and S. Anthony Baron, Ph.D.

Library of Congress Cataloging-in-Publication Data

Wheeler, Eugene D.
  Violence in schools, hospitals, and public places : a prevention and management guide / by Eugene D. Wheeler and S. Anthony Baron.
      p.   cm.
  Includes bibliographical references and index.
    ISBN 0-934793-52-2 : $22.95. — ISBN 0-934793-51-4 (pbk.) : $14.95
    1. Violence—United States. 2. Violence—United States-
-Prevention. 3. School violence—United States. 4. Violence in
hospitals—United States. I. Baron, S. Anthony, 1955-
II. Title.
HN90.V5W48   1993
303.6'0973—dc20   93-35552
                                                        CIP

DEDICATION

**TO THE VICTIMS AND THEIR FAMILIES
WHO HAVE SUFFERED FROM THE ACTS
OF VIOLENT PERPETRATORS**

ACKNOWLEDGMENTS

The authors wish to thank the many people and organizations that contributed information, data, reviewed the manuscript, and made suggestions for improving the book.

Courts
Charlotte Westover, National Center for State Courts
Judge Bert Hensen
National Sheriffs Association

Schools, K-12
George Butterfield, Deputy Director, & staff, National School Safety Center
Charlotte McElroy, Principal, Anacapa Middle School
Little Rock School District, Arkansas

Colleges and Universities
Eileen Stevens, C.H.U.C.K., Committee to Halt Useless College Killings
Connie Clery, Security on Campus, Inc.
Towson University Campus Violence Prevention Center

Government
Suzanne Schroeder, California State Employment Development Department
U.S. Dept. Health & Human Services, Occupational Safety & Health
U.S. Dept. of Justice, Bureau of Justice Statistics
California State Dept. of Motor Vehicles
California State Dept. of Social Services

Hospitals
Marilyn Stoner, RN, BSN, author and nurse educator
Linda Glasson, Director, Safety/Security, International Association for Healthcare Security & Safety
Nigel Keep, RN, CEN, MICN, Co-author of AB 508
Colleen Scott, Ventura Community Memorial Hospital
San Gorgonio Memorial Hospital

James Packer, MD, Emergency Dept. Physician, Sharp Chula Vista Medical Center
California Association of Hospitals
California Emergency Room Nurses Association
New York State Emergency Room Nurses Association

Security
James P. Graham, Certified Protection Professional, FBI, (ret), James P. Graham & Associates
Robert Owen, Police Chief (ret.), Oxnard Police Dept.
Frank Egan, Crime Prevention Officer (ret.), Oxnard Police Dept.

Victims/Gun Control
Anne Seymour, Director of Communications &Resource Development, and Gary W. Markham, National Victim Center, Arlington, VA
National Victim Center, Ft. Worth, TX
Janice Harris Lord, MADD
National Victims Resource Center
Coalition to Stop Gun Violence

Human Resources
Kathleen A. Wheeler, Ph.D., Sharp Chula Vista Medical Center
Bobbi Cornelius, Dir. Human Resources, Jenny Craig International

Editing
Kathleen Sublette
Eugenie G. Wheeler
Lou Hartney
Kathy Stinson

Eugene D. Wheeler & S. Anthony Baron, Ph.D.
September 1993

TABLE OF CONTENTS

DISCLAIMER

This publication is designed to provide accurate and authoritative information in regard to the subject matter covered. It is sold with the understanding that the publisher is not engaged in redering security, psychological, medical, or other professional services. If expert assistance or counseling is needed, the services of a competent professional should be sought.

INTRODUCTION

Violence has penetrated our workplaces; schools, universities, hospitals, clinics, government offices, courts, libraries, parks, and even little league games. This is not violence for economic gain, but violence to strike back, to get even, to punish a person or an organization for slow or bad service, for some perceived wrong.

The weapons most used for these vengeful acts are guns; hand guns, machine guns, and assault guns. As a result thousands of people are getting killed and wounded.

Americans have a right to go to school or college and learn in a pleasant and safe environment. We should be able to receive care in a hospital without fear of being shot. We should be able to go to our place of work without fear of assault. We should be able to enter courts, government agencies, or libraries without fear of verbal or bodily attack. We could once visit these places without fear, but no longer.

Murder in the workplace is one of the fastest growing types of homicide in the United States. It is the most frequent cause of death in the workplace for women and second for men.

In addition to the human cost of violence to employees, patients, students, and their families, organizations and campuses suffer greater economic costs, disruption of operations, increased legal fees, medical expenses, and loss of productivity.

It is time for Americans to call a halt to the unnecessary slaughter taking place and the fear that it generates. This book is written to show the extent of violence nationwide, and its impact on the people who work and utilize these important organizations; places of work, study, government, care, and play. We want you to see who the perpetrators are, and to understand some of the causes of the violence in our society. But most important, we want you to believe that something can be done to stem the tide of this assault on our society. Goal setting and planning must take place. We indicate how individuals, groups, staffs and managers of organizations, and legislators can take action that can prevent violence or facilitate the healing process should it occur.

Violence in the United States is deterring foreign tourists from visiting. Many of those that come here take courses on protecting themselves from criminal elements.

This book is written to show that as a nation we can bring about desirable change, but it will take a concerted effort by all of us. Many outstanding groups are taking positive action. But they need help. We hope our book sheds light on the seriousness of the problem, shows steps that you can take to bring about change, and stimulates you to action.

PART I

A NATIONAL PROFILE OF VIOLENCE

CHAPTER 1

VIOLENCE IN SCHOOLS, K – 12

HIGH SCHOOLS

Reseda (California) High School

A dozen teenagers watched as a fifteen-year-old student shot and killed a seventeen-year-old classmate at Reseda High School in February of 1993. Robert Heard, a Reseda High football player, confronted Michael Shean Ensley in a corridor during a midmorning snack break. He fired once, hitting Ensley in the chest. Ensley staggered outside and collapsed in a grassy quadrangle area near the administration office. Several who witnessed the incident initially thought it was play acting, but rushed the injured youth to the nurse's office when they realized he was hurt. He was pronounced dead at Northridge Hospital Medical Center a short time later.

Heard then fled the campus but was apprehended shortly afterward without a struggle by a school police officer. He was carrying a small-caliber handgun. Both the perpetrator and his victim were boys bussed to Reseda High's suburban campus. Ensley's mother said later that he had enrolled at Reseda to escape the violence of South Central Los Angeles urban gangs. After the incident, several students expressed fears about returning to their classes.

The Los Angeles Police declined to characterize the shooting as gang related, but both boys were involved in "tagging," or marking property with graffiti. Prior to the shooting they became involved in an argument in the hallway about differences between the tagging crews. School administrators explained that both boys had school discipline problems and were affiliated with cliques of students who party and hang out together. Despite conflicting stories of whether the boys were involved in gangs or tagging groups, both youths were classified by school authorities as "opportunity transfers," students who are transferred to another school for disciplinary problems. When this happens, often the new school is not notified of previous difficulties.

The school administration quickly brought in a crisis team consisting of school psychologists, counselors, nurses, and administrators who have developed a specialty in counseling students and teachers when a tragedy occurs.

Fairfax (California) High School

"The shot seemed to come out of nowhere," said Fairfax High School teacher, Charles Schwartz. He added that even the suspected shooter seemed surprised. In January of 1993, a fifteen-year old boy, carrying a .357-caliber Magnum in his backpack, shot a classmate to death and wounded another during an early morning English class. The suspect was a student from Audubon Junior High School who was attending a special winter break class at Fairfax High. While handling the gun inside his knapsack a bullet fired and went through the chest of seventeen-year old Eli Kogman, sitting one desk away. It also pierced the side of sixteen-year old Demetrius Rice who was returning to his seat from the teacher's desk.

"There were no arguments," teacher Schwartz said. "There was nothing to indicate that anything was wrong." While other students were whisked from the room, the perpetrator rushed to the side of the wounded Kogman after the gun fired and then stood bewildered beside his desk, murmuring: "I'm sorry, I'm sorry." His name was not revealed because of his age, but he told police and school officials that he carried the gun in his book bag to protect himself on the RTD bus he rode to and from school each day.

When Mr. Schwartz approached the youth, he gave up his weapon without resistance. Fortunately, Eli Kogman was only wounded and recovered. Demetrius Rice was not so lucky. The life of this young student and aspiring football player came to an abrupt, untimely end.

The teacher explained that the suspect had problems and was failing the class—a freshman remedial English course intended for students who needed extra help. He had often refused to do his work in class, disrupted lessons by talking with classmates, and insulted and challenged the teacher. The teacher had held an amicable consultation with the boy's parents and believed that an effort to improve was being made prior to the shooting incident.

According to investigators it appeared that the student had been carrying the gun to and from school for several days. Several other students said the youth had previously bragged about having the weapon.

WEAPONS IN SCHOOLS

Los Angeles Unified School District (LAUSD)

The above incidents renewed the debate over how best to protect students at school. While some school officials downplay the prevalence of campus killings as rare experiences, the statistics indicate otherwise. During the 1991-92 school year, 1,403 weapons—including 405 guns—were confiscated at school facilities in the 640,000 student LAUSD. The number of guns discovered at schools was up about 17 percent from the previous year. Of the guns found, 33 were taken in elementary school, 158 in junior high school, and 182 from senior high school students. More weapons are taken to school but are not found by authorities.

Guns In Schools, Nationally

The U.S. Department of Justice and the National School Safety Center (NSSC) estimates that about 100,000 students across the country bring guns to school every day. The National Education Association (NEA) called on the federal government to increase spending for school security, including metal detectors, counseling, and other programs to reduce campus crime.

New York City School District

The combination of easy access to handguns and other firearms and the use of violence to settle disputes, particularly among our youth, has shown its effect within the New York City Public School System. Because of the potential harm to victims, the Division of School Safety tracks weapons.

In the first category, weapons and unauthorized items confiscated from students in schools or found on school grounds numbered approximately 2,737 for the first eight months of the 1991/92 school year. These weapons were taken through the metal detection program. They include guns, box cutters, knives, razors and other potentially dangerous instruments. The program was used in 300 intermediate schools and approximately 1,300 high schools.

The second category of weapons tracked are those taken during incidents that occur in schools not involving metal detection programs. During the 1990/91 school year, 2,983 weapons and other unauthorized items were confiscated from students by security staff in the schools and safe schools teams.

In the first seven months of the 1992 school year, 1,713 weapons were taken from students:

Handguns 97
Rifles 4
Ammunition 41
Air guns 63
Explosives 7
Chemicals 33
Imitation pistols 50
Dangerous knives 870
Dangerous instruments 548

California's School Crime

In the 1988-89 school year, 174,478 crimes were reported in California schools, up five percent from the previous year. Assaults were up 16 percent to 69,191. Armed assaults were up 25 percent to 1,830. The increase in guns on campus jumped 40 percent over the previous year.

JUNIOR HIGH SCHOOLS

Incidents of violence were on the rise in junior high schools in the LAUSD as well as in the high schools. Some of the violent incidents occurring in junior high schools were:

- In September 1991, a young boy was hit in the back by shots fired from a passing vehicle near Muir Junior High School in South Los Angeles.

- In July 1991, a fourteen-year old boy was shot in the leg trying to flee from two gang members who came on campus at Compton's Enterprise Middle School.

- In May 1991, a fourteen-year old gang member was shot to death in front of Millikan Junior High School in Sherman Oaks.

- In April 1991, an 11-year-old boy was killed in the schoolyard of Ralph J. Bunche Middle School in Compton.

METAL DETECTORS

Increasing violence has caused school organizations to rethink the reports of positive experience and improvement in weapon control reported by New York City and other school districts in the nation who have been using metal detectors. Some fifty school districts across the country who use detectors report that they help deter weapons on campus.

Compelled by the accidental shootings at Fairfax and Reseda High Schools, the Los Angeles Board of Education followed the lead of other districts like New York and Chicago and began using hand-held metal detectors at high schools and middle schools. The detectors are used on a random basis without warning to students. The LAUSD also mandated that any student caught with a gun on campus be expelled. Under the new policy any student carrying any sort of gun, or even a realistic replica, faces expulsion for the rest of that semester and the next. The LAUSD expelled nearly 100 students for carrying weapons on the school grounds in 1990 and 1991.

ELEMENTARY SCHOOLS

While the majority of incidents involve high school and middle school age students, elementary schools are also experiencing violence. The following represent only a few of the thousands of incidents occurring.

Greenwood, South Carolina

Oakland Elementary School in Greenwood, South Carolina, was the scene of a tragic scenario of on-campus violence in September of 1988. While first graders were eating lunch, a man entered the school cafeteria through the front door and started shooting, wounding one teacher and three students. He left that building, reloaded his gun, and entered a third grade classroom where he again emptied the gun at students. One third grader died in the school and another died three days later. Nine persons, including two teachers, were wounded during the violence. It is a wonder that more students were not killed.

The incident happened so quickly that while some students were escaping through windows, classes were still in progress in other parts of the building. Students ran into nearby woods, across streets into neighborhood yards, and anywhere that offered safety as awareness of the emergency spread. The gunman was captured by school personnel within minutes. School personnel then had the task of finding and accounting for all their students. Student groups were formed on the front lawn so parents could find their children. The gunman was taken into custody by the police less than two hours after the shooting began. All the students were sent home except those who had been taken for medical treatment.

Aftermath

To assist the school staff in dealing with their feelings and emotions, professional counselors were brought in. The counselors helped students deal with their fears, both individually and in groups. After two days, school officials invited parents and their children back to the school for an afternoon open house. By taking groups on a walking tour of the campus, parents and students were assured that the school was physically back to normal.

School classes were resumed on the third day after the incident. Counselors coached teachers to help students talk about or act out feelings about the tragedy. Anyone who had fears was encouraged to express them. Police and parents were made highly visible as open symbols of safety and security. Individuals, businesses, and the entire community provided special activities and treats in an effort to help the students and teachers feel safe in their school.

Columbus, Georgia

Apparently angered because their teacher tried to discipline them, seven sixth-graders planned to murder her. The 12-and 13-year-old students, four boys and three girls, from the Georgetown Elementary School were arrested and charged with disorderly conduct and released to their parents. They plotted for months to dump chemicals in her iced tea, tried to trip her on stairs, and took weapons to school. Detective Maj. John Wood said that the students conspired "to do away with [their teacher] because she wanted to make them behave." One girl brought chemicals to school from her home chemistry set and one of the boys brought a handgun to school in his book bag.

Stockton, California

On January 17, 1989, a man carrying an AK-47 semi-automatic assault rifle walked onto the Cleveland Elementary School playground in Stockton, California, and opened fire. Five children and the gunman were dead less than five minutes later. Twenty-nine other students and a teacher were wounded, 15 seriously. This shooting claimed more lives than any other schoolyard attack in history.

Sylmar, California

An eleven-year-old boy threatened a classmate with an unloaded BB pistol in March, 1993, at Herrick Avenue Elementary School in Sylmar, California. He was expelled in an act reflecting the tougher gun control laws enacted by the Los Angeles Unified School District. Police explained that the youth pulled out the pistol, pointed it at a female classmate, and told her that he was going to kill her and her family.

Los Angeles Board of Education Expulsion Policies

Shortly after the adoption of toughened expulsion policies following the Fairfax High incident, the Los Angeles Board expelled 13 teenagers for bringing guns to school. Sixteen had been previously dropped from the system, including a 12-year-old middle school student who carried a BB gun.

While some officials expressed concern over the effect of expelling such a young student, parents and friends of previously slain high school students begged the school board in an impassioned speech to find "sensible solutions to this monstrous problem" of school violence. "Violence is not just a problem at our schools," they explained. "It's a household problem, a community problem, a city problem." The board convened another task force to address the issue of "opportunity transfers," or transfers of students with disciplinary problems. "Something is wrong and we need to examine this thoroughly," said school board member Julie Korenstein. "We can't keep shuffling these kids around the district and never solve the problem."

NATIONWIDE SCHOOL VIOLENCE

School violence has infected school districts across the country.

Chicago, Illinois — In March of 1992, an eight-year-old boy brought a gun to school in his book bag. Thinking it was a toy, he shot and paralyzed an eight-year-old girl in the classroom.

Baltimore, Maryland — In February of 1992, at Roland Park Elementary/Middle School, a seventh grader shot a school police officer for confiscating his pager.

Winnetka, Illinois — A woman walked into a classroom at the Hubbard Woods Elementary School in May of 1988, killed an eight-year-old boy and wounded six others.

Cokeville, Wyoming—In May of 1986 a man and woman held a group of students and teachers hostage in Cokeville Elementary School. The bomb they brought into the building exploded accidentally, killing the woman and burning some of the hostages. The man then committed suicide after shooting one teacher in the back.

Palo Duro High School, Amarillo, Texas—September 1992—A teenager shot six students in school after a fight; two were seriously hurt.

Lindhurst High School, Olivehurst, California, May, 1992—Eric Houston, 22, angry with a teacher who gave him an failing grade that kept him from graduating, walked onto the campus and shot and killed the teacher, Robert Brens, and three students. He was armed with a shotgun and rifle. He injured 11 other students and held 59 students and teachers hostage during an eight-hour siege.

Largo High School, Washington, D.C.—March 1992—A female classmate stabbed a 16-year-old girl in the abdomen with a three-inch paring knife.

Thomas Jefferson High School, Brooklyn, New York—February, 1992, While students were changing classes, a ninth-grader fatally shot two students in a school hallway.

PRE-SCHOOL

Neuilly-Sur-Seine, France

The French too, have experienced violence in their schools. On a sunny morning at 10 a.m., a hooded man, claiming to be armed with explosives, took a class of three and four-year-old children hostage in Neuilly-Sur-Seine in May of 1993. He demanded a multimillion franc ransom and threatened to blow up the pre-school if his demand was not met. Early that morning, the perpetrator handed authorities a message stating that he would "rather die than be captured alive." This drama, the first of its type in modern France, took place in an unlikely setting. Neuilly is a wealthy Paris suburb and its residents include many foreign nationals, including Americans. The suburb takes special pride in its low crime rate and safe streets.

After about four hours of siege, as hungry toddlers started crying, the man was persuaded to release eight of the children in return for milk and sandwiches. He later released another child and let a doctor into the room. In the morning, six more children were released. Students from the rest of the Commandant Charcot school were evacuated from classrooms and released to their parents, but the perpetrator kept a handful of pre-schoolers hostage.

The teacher, by acting as though the perpetrator was a repairman, and reading and singing with the children, kept them calm. On the second day when the perpetrator fell asleep, police stormed the classroom and shot the man to death. All the children were rescued safely. The teacher became a national heroine for keeping the children composed and helping to prevent chaos. The French began to wonder if American-style violence was reaching their country.

GROWTH OF SCHOOL VIOLENCE

When the findings of the Safe School Study Report, "Violent Schools - Safe Schools" were released to Congress in 1978, the National Institute of Education (NIE) pointed out some shocking statistics about crime on the nation's elementary and secondary school campuses.

- Approximately 282,000 students (1.3 percent) are physically attacked in America's secondary schools each month.

- About 2.4 million (11 percent) have something stolen from them in a typical month.

- Almost eight percent of urban junior and senior high school students miss at least one day of classes a month because they are afraid to go to school.

- Over 25 percent of all schools are subject to vandalism in a given month.

- Ten percent of schools are burglarized. The annual cost of school crime was estimated at around $200 million.

The National Crime Survey (May 1991) reported that nearly three million thefts and violent crimes occur on or near school campuses every year, which is almost 16,000 incidents per school day.

BUREAU OF JUSTICE STATISTICS REPORT ON "TEENAGE VICTIMS"

While a safe schools study on the scale of the NIE study has not been conducted since 1978, national, state, and local studies confirm that crime and violence are more serious problems in the 1990s. "Teenage Victims," the Bureau of Justice Statistics (BJS) report, released in May 1991, estimates that 1.9 million violent victimizations are sustained by 18.1 million teenagers each year (1985 through 1988). In interviews conducted from a nationwide sample of about 50,000 households, the study found:

- Teenagers were much more likely than adults to be victims of crimes of violence.

- On the average, every 1,000 teenagers experienced 67 violent crimes each year, compared to 16 for every 1,000 adults age 20 or older.

- About half of all violent crimes and 63 percent of crimes of theft against teens age 12 to 19 took place on the street, in a school building, or on school property.

- Adolescents age 12 to 15 were about twice as likely as older teens to experience crimes in a school building or on school property. About 37 percent of violent crimes and 81 percent of crimes of theft against younger teenagers occurred at school, compared with 17 percent of the violent crimes and 39 percent of the crimes of theft against older teens.

URBAN vs RURAL VIOLENCE

A 1990 Texas A & M University study indicates that many rural public schools, especially those near large cities, have worse violence problems than the national average.the study included 1,004 eighth and tenth grade students from 23 small Central Texas communities. The significant findings showed:

- Thirty-four percent of students report having been threatened with bodily harm, though not actually hurt, at school or on a school bus. Fifteen percent claimed they had something taken from them by force or threat of bodily harm. Fourteen percent said they had been physically attacked and six percent admitted that someone tried to force them to have sex.

- Half of the boys and twenty-eight percent of the girls were in at least one fight during the previous year.

- More than half said they had not received instruction in school on ways to avoid fighting and violence.

- Students believe they should fight if someone hits them (78 percent), hurts someone they care about (74 percent), insults their family (58 percent), or breaks something they own on purpose (53 percent).

- More than twenty percent said that threatening to use a weapon would help prevent fights. Nearly 17 percent thought "acting tough" would deter altercations.

THE CRIME CONTROL ACT

The Crime Control Act of 1990 was passed by Congress in an effort to regain control of schools in America. The act prohibits the possession or discharge of a firearm on or within 1000 feet of private, parochial or public school grounds. Violation calls for up to five years imprisonment, a fine of not more than $250,000, or both. The act exempts guns properly stored in automobiles (i.e., unloaded and locked in gun racks), in homes within 1,000 feet of school grounds and carried on hunting leases near school property.

Two states, California and Florida, have passed laws making adults who own guns criminally liable for shootings committed by children who have access to the weapons. A maximum of three years in prison can result for a fatal shooting that occurs. A similar law was passed in Florida after a 1988 survey conducted by the Florida School Boards Association and the Association of School Administrators in a survey on the use of guns in schools found that nearly 93 percent of the weapons brought to school came from the homes of students or from homes of friends or relatives.

CHANGING NATURE OF SCHOOL PROBLEMS

Today, the problems in our schools are guns, weapons, substance abuse, and gangs. Many people equate school violence with large urban areas such as New York, Chicago or Los Angeles. However, violence has invaded suburban and rural schools too. Not only big-city schools, but also private schools are involved. House of Representatives Bill 4538 introduced the "Classroom Safety Act of 1992," summarizing the rising tide of violence in America's schools:

- Nearly 3,000,000 crimes occur on or near school campuses every year.

- One-fourth of the major school districts now use metal detectors in an attempt to reduce the number of weapons brought into schools by students.

- Twenty percent of teachers report being threatened by violence by students.

- The despair brought on by poverty and disenfranchisement that affects millions of our youth is rapidly entering the schools.

- Schools are being asked to take on responsibilities that society as a whole has neglected, forcing teachers to referee fights rather than teach.

- Teachers are staging walk-outs to protest the violence which denies interested students the opportunity to learn.

No longer is there an assurance of safety. Violence in America's schools has increased dramatically over the past decade and continues to escalate.

From a "Youth Risk Behavior Survey" conducted by the Centers for Disease Control, of a sample of 11,631 high school students throughout the United States, Puerto Rico and the Virgin Islands, 19.6 percent of students had carried a weapon during the preceding 30 days. From newspaper accounts alone, the Center to Prevent Handgun Violence reported that 65 students were killed, 186 wounded, six school employees died, and 15 were injured during the four academic years of 1986 through 1990.

WHY STUDENTS CARRY GUNS

A 1990 National Center for Education Statistics survey indicated that 21 percent of 25,000 eight graders from 1,000 public and private schools reported they had witnessed weapons at school. Students bring weapons to school because it gives them a sense of security. When asked why they bring guns students offer answers such as:

... because I feel threatened and intimidated

. . . to make people think I'm a drug dealer

. . . because I need to have status

. . . to save my own life

. . . I feel I need protection . . . Maybe I'm a cynic, but I'm a realist.

How Children Obtain Weapons

Despite new laws governing unsafe storage of guns that are accessible to those younger than 14, home is where guns are primarily obtained by young people. Students perceive themselves as potential victims, and in certain cases, feel that a gun is needed for protection. High school students indicate that they need guns and other weapons for protection.

In 1992, in Houston, Texas, school administrators learned that one of their students was running a gun rental service on campus. In Oakland, California, students told of their biggest fear — getting to school through drug-dealing/gang infested territory. Carrying a weapon, for many, is seen as a means of survival.

Weapons include any object that can inflict injury upon an assailant such as guns, razor blades, brass knuckles, clubs, broken glass, wire, or other pointed instruments. Ammunition, chemicals, and explosives are used because they are accessible.

DRUGS

The impact of gangs and the presence of drugs are directly related to the increase of weapons in schools according to the Center to Prevent Handgun Violence. Over 18 percent of all weapons in school incidents are drug or gang-related, 15 percent involve long-standing disagreements, 13 percent involve playing with or cleaning guns, 12 percent involve romantic disagreements, and 10 percent involve fights and material possessions. More than 13 percent of convicted offenders, including teenagers, held in local jails during 1989 claimed they had committed their crime for money to support their drug habit. Eighteen percent admitted to being under the influence of a major drug at the time of the offense.

In addition, there is a growing underground market for weapons stolen from gun dealers, businesses, cars, and homes. A common source of stolen weapons is drug addicts. In Los Angeles, California, the riots of 1992 sparked a record year for gun sales, both legally and illegally. Over 4,000 guns were stolen during the civil unrest and many of them ended up in the hands of teenagers.

GANGS

Since younger gang members attend school, it has become a prime recruiting ground. Gang members stake out their turfs in their territory, including school grounds. It was recently estimated that New York City has 50 gangs with 5,000 members. Chicago has 125 gangs with 12,500 members; Dallas 225 gangs, and Los Angeles, more than 900 gangs with about 100,000 members. Gangs are not just a big city or inner city problem, and membership crosses racial and ethnic boundaries.

Across the country, many programs to combat gang related crimes have been formed. Often, school administrators and parents do not want to admit that their students or children are involved in gangs. But to get control of gangs, it is imperative that school administrators establish clear behavior guidelines and specifically prohibit gang activity. Ventura County, California, police agencies have developed guidelines for identifying youths as potential gang members. Exhibiting one of these characteristics will label a youth to be a gang "wanna-be" or "hanger-on." Two can result in a youth being labeled as "associate" gang member. Displaying five or more of these attributes can cause police to label someone as a hard-core gang member.

The criteria include:

- Having gang tatoos
- Wearing gang garb that could include the color of clothing, types of clothing, head covering or methods of grooming
- Displaying gang markings or slogans
- Possessing literature that indicates gang membership
- Admitting gang membership
- Being arrested with known gang members
- Attending functions sponsored by gangs
- Obtaining information from a reliable informant
- Getting statements from relatives identifying the youth as a gang member
- Receiving information from other law enforcement agencies that a youth is a gang member
- Exhibiting behavior fitting police profiles of gang related drug dealing
- Being stopped by police with a known gang member
- Loitering, riding or meeting with a gang member
- Selling or distributing drugs for a known gang member
- Helping a known gang member commit a crime

If students are identified as gang members, many local police work with schools and other youth programs to change their behavior before violence or the breaking of laws occur.

TEACHER VICTIMIZATION

Students are not the only ones being victimized at school. Nearly 5,200 of the nation's million secondary school teachers are physically attacked at school each month, according to a National Institute of Education (NIE) study. About 1,000 are hurt seriously enough to require medical attention. Theft is reported by 130,000 teachers in a month's time. Having something taken from them by force, weapons or threats, is reported by 6,000 teachers.

In Chicago, the Criminal Justice Information Authority reports that one in 11 teachers in Illinois high schools reported that a student had threatened to hurt them during the month preceding the survey. More than half reported that a student had used obscenity and a third reported that a student had made an obscene gesture at them.

In a 1987 survey, "Public School Teachers' Perspectives on School Discipline," it was revealed that almost 20 percent of teachers polled indicated that they had been threatened at some time, and eight percent had been threatened in the last 12 months.

Additional results of the above survey report on the apprehensive attitudes of many of today's teachers. Forty-four percent of teachers in public schools reported that there was more disruptive classroom behavior in their schools in 1986-87 than five years earlier. Elementary school teachers reported that disruptive behavior had increased. Twenty-nine percent of teachers indicated that they had seriously considered leaving teaching because of student misbehavior, and 17 percent reported they had seriously considered leaving in the last 12 months.

In 1987, a study of teachers' perspectives on student discipline by the Office of Educational Research and Improvement (OERI), reported the following frustrations experienced by elementary and secondary school teachers:

- Teachers estimated that about seven percent of the students they taught were habitual behavior problems.

- The most frequently rated factors limiting the ability of teachers to maintain order was lack of alternative placement (39 percent) and lack of student interest (38 percent).

- Seventeen percent of teachers rated administrator fear of being sued and 14 percent rated teacher fear of being sued as greatly limiting their effort to maintain order.

- One-third regarded their schools' discipline policy as not strict enough. Twenty-eight percent regarded the policy as not comprehensive enough and 50 percent indicated it was not consistently applied.

- Teachers rated increased student self-discipline developed at home (74 percent), smaller classes (63 percent), and increased parental support (62 percent) as "very productive" in improving school discipline.

UNREPORTED CRIME

Many crimes that occur in school are not reported to the police. Administrators fear that reporting incidents may cause them to look ineffective or incompetent. Also, political factions within communities may actually discourage accurate reporting of school crimes. According to information in "Teenage Victims," in 1991, 37 percent of the violent crimes in school buildings and 32 percent of those on school property were not reported to the police primarily because the crime was reported to someone else.

The Illinois Criminal Justice Information Authority also reported that school crimes against both students and teachers are often not reported to any authorities. During the 1989-90 school year, nearly one-third of student robberies, one-fourth of thefts and 40 percent of assaults were not reported. Among teachers, 16 percent of robberies, 40 percent of thefts, and 25 percent of assaults were not reported.

IMPACT OF MEDIA VIOLENCE

Many children have been anesthetized to violence by the programs they see presented on television and in the movies. They witness thousands of murders and other violent acts before they reach high school age. The American Psychological Association estimates the average TV watcher/movie-going American child will witness 8,000 murders and 100,000 other acts of violence by the time he reaches the seventh grade. According to Dr. Louis Simpson, a psychiatrist who counsels inner-city gang members in Los Angeles, "Shootings involving teenagers will not be reduced until something is done about the proliferation of violence in the media. It's like a Shakespeare play where the characters have no control over the tragedies that will occur in their lives," he said. "Life has no meaning."

The desire to own a gun extends beyond the need for revenge or protection to the desire for status and glamour for many youths. "They are like the latest Air Jordan sneakers," Simpson said. Rap music and street language add to the allure of weapons. A gun is a *heater, strap, nine, burner* or *gat* on the streets. Often, the lyrics to several songs advocate violence against the police or other ethnic groups.

LEGAL PROBLEMS

There is economic and legal justification for spending funds for security. If school districts don't take action, they may face serious legal costs. Unfortunately, when they do take action they may also be thwarted by lawsuits. There are several legal problems that can arise from a crisis or the efforts to prevent one as illustrated in recent court cases.

In *Hosemann v. Oakland Unified School District*, Stephen Hosemann argued that he was physically assaulted on his junior high school campus by a former classmate. He further argued that school officials failed to protect him even though they were aware of threats against him. The court found in May 1986 that the school district and supervisors were liable for Hosemann's injuries and ordered the district to develop a security plan for its campuses. Even though the ruling was reversed in 1989 by an appellate court, the need for legislative action to make schools safer was still reinforced.

The case of *New Jersey v. T.L.O.*, concerning searches of students on campus, went all the way to the Supreme Court where it was concluded that school officials do not have to conform to the same stringent standard required of law enforcement personnel; they do not need to obtain a warrant or reach the standard of probable cause before searching a student. The court ruled that school officials must have "reasonable grounds" to suspect a search would turn up evidence that the student had violated the law or the school's rules.

These are just two examples of cases brought against school districts but many other similar suits have been filed. Administrators should examine their security systems closely to protect their schools from being liable in a court case if they can show that they exercised due diligence in preventing violence and crime on their campuses.

RIGHT TO VIOLENCE-FREE SCHOOLS

What can be done to provide a safer school environment? What does the public have a right to expect? In the National School Safety Center (NSSC) Resource Paper, *School Crisis Prevention and Response,* it is noted that courts have held that schools are expected to provide a physical environment conducive to the purposes of an educational institution, although a school may not be expected to insure nor guarantee the safety of its students. This finding is appropriate on campuses where educators are charged with the custody, care and control of students' behavior. The right to safe schools includes the right of students and staff to:

- Protection against foreseeable criminal activities
- Protection against violence or student crime which adequate supervision can prevent
- Protection against potentially dangerous students who are identifiable
- Protection against dangerous persons admitted to school in a negligent manner
- Protection from negligently selected, retained, or trained school administrators, teachers or staff

VIOLENCE PREVENTION POLICY FOR SCHOOLS, K-12

The NSSC, in its resource paper *School Crisis Prevention & Response*, recommends that a security plan be prepared and that the following general security measures be taken to lessen the chances of violence on campus:

- A local school security committee or task force comprised of school officials should be established by school districts. Planning for needed safety measures and their implementation should be performed by this task force, including regular review of safety and security measures.
- "Crime-resistant savvy" should be developed and greater responsibility taken by school administrators in working with the school board and districts.
- A comprehensive crisis management plan should be developed by schools which incorporates resources available through other community agencies.
- Regular updates on safety plans and in-service training should be conducted to keep school staff informed. The training should include certified staff,

classified staff, part-time employees, and substitute teachers.

- Volunteers from the community, as well as parents, should be used to help patrol surrounding neighborhoods and supervise the campus before, during, and after school.

- Access points to school campuses should be monitored during the school day. Access should be limited where possible. A single visitor entrance should be monitored by a receptionist or security officer and visitors should be required to sign in and wear an identification pass. Delivery entrances should also be monitored closely.

- Students should be taught to report suspicious individuals or unusual activity. They should also be taught to take responsibility for their own safety by learning personal safety and conflict-resolution techniques.

- A curriculum committee focusing on teaching students non-violence, pro-social skills, conflict-resolution, law-related education, and good decision making should be established.

- Plans should be made to establish alternative schools to handle problem students. When these offenders are expelled from school there must be other programs in place to keep them off the streets where other violent incidents may be perpetrated.

The implementation of any good security program presents a great challenge to school administrators to address legitimate fears without going to extremes that damage campus academic atmosphere.

METHODS TO PREVENT SCHOOL VIOLENCE

PHYSICAL SECURITY PLAN

Each school should prepare a Physical Security Plan to fit its particular situation and location in the community. To help school officials, a suggested outline entitled "School Security Plan for Schools and Colleges" is located in Appendix I. The outline covers doors, windows, other openings and outbuildings, control of keys, lighting, grounds, landscaping visibility and access, access control procedures for visitors, students and staff, property identification and inventory control, alarms, and general school security policy.

Some General Methods To Prevent Violence Are:

Hold emergency drills — Before the shooting in Cleveland Elementary School in Stockton, California, occurred, school officials held frequent emergency drills, which helped when a real crisis occurred. Principal Patricia Busher said, "All children must be taught that if they are on the playground or in the classroom and something makes them uncomfortable or unsafe, they need to look for the first adult and follow their directions." When the shooting occurred at Cleveland School, there was no hysterical behavior on the part of the children. Even though they were very frightened, they followed the directions of the adults.

Establish Neighborhood Watch Programs — Parents and volunteers should patrol nearby campus areas and report any suspicious behavior. Ask for community members to volunteer their homes as safe places where children can go if they are threatened on the street or at a bus stop.

Maintain clean grounds and buildings — This will eliminate possible hiding places. After improving lighting and trimming back bushes, installing emergency telephone call boxes, and instituting a campus watch, violent crime on the University of Virginia, Charlottesville, campus dropped 38 percent. Property crime decreased 47 percent.

Establish a Crime Prevention Club — One school offered monetary awards of $20 to $25 to students who gave accurate tips on weapons in schools (while maintaining the student's confidentiality). Other schools have established a toll free telephone number which ensures confidentiality to report weapons on campus.

Environmental Design — When a district plans a new school, architectural design should take security issues into account. Evaluate physical space by using the "Three-Ds" guidelines offered by Timothy D. Crowe, author of *Crime Prevention Through Environmental Design*: Designation, Definition and Design. Does the space clearly belong to someone or some group? Is its use clearly defined? Does the physical design match the intended use? Can normal users naturally control the activities, control access, and provide for surveillance if necessary?

CRISIS PLAN

Despite taking careful security precautions, the unthinkable can occur — a bomb threat turns out to be real, an individual with a gun intrudes on a campus. The next most important step a school should take is to develop a **written crisis plan** and to familiarize school staff with it. Each school and school district should have policies regarding visitors, communication, and evacuation. The suggestions that follow are suggested by the NSSC and have been implemented by some school districts that faced a crisis in the past. Assign clear roles. Personnel should be designated to:

1. Go to the hospital or emergency medical site with injured students.

2. Oversee computer and telephone datalines.

3. Inform other school administrators about the emergency and how it is being dealt with.

4. Work with the media.

5. Handle transportation needs.

6. Assist in identifying students and adults who are injured or killed.

7. Review personnel and student records and notify family.

COMMUNICATIONS

One of the most critical areas that exists in an emergency is communication. Rumors can multiply quickly and panic students in tense situations. School officials should communicate accurate information to students, parents, staff, law enforcement personnel, medical services, the media and hospitals. Depending on the nature of the crisis, the following suggestions could prove vital.

1. Designate at least one private unlisted telephone line for official use during an emergency.

2. Have alternative communication systems available if possible, such as a fax machine, a computer with a modem, and RJ11 telephone jacks.

3. Have a portable telephone to use in case phone lines are down.

4. Keep a working bullhorn to be used to communicate to large groups.

5. Establish a computer-based bulletin board system (BBS) that can be used through telephone modems.

6. Assemble an emergency communication kit which includes a list of emergency telephone numbers, a telephone directory, a fax machine and computer telephone numbers.

7. In case of a bomb threat, telephone recording equipment to record the threat would be a great help.

8. Two-way radios to communicate with school personnel should be made available. Radios should not be used in case of a bomb threat as they may detonate electric blasting caps.

TRANSPORTATION

1. Include bus drivers in staff security training programs.

2. Keep an emergency information kit with writing paper, pens, pencils, and a list of students who ride the bus for each route with each driver.

IDENTIFICATION

1. ID Badges should be made for all school personnel who will be involved in emergency crisis situations.

2. A list of any injured students or adults should be kept when they are moved to a hospital or other medical center.

3. Teachers should be trained to take their class rosters or grade books with them if they must leave the building in an emergency. Make plans for teachers and students to meet in a specific place on campus.

4. Establish a plan to release children to their parents or guardians after an emergency. Mass hysteria can occur if this is not controlled. It is a good idea to "sign out" children to their parents or guardians to maintain a record.

DEALING WITH THE MEDIA

A media spokesperson should be appointed who should follow the the suggestions below which involve preplanning:

- Keep statements brief and cover only the facts.
- Maintain a positive attitude. The public has a right to know and a need to understand what has happened.
- Ignore abrasive statements by press personalities.

- Compile a list of media representatives and have a stack of envelopes ready to mail press releases.
- Develop a fact sheet about the school and district for a handout.
- Maintain an adequate supply of news release forms.
- Identify areas where reporters can congregate and/or news conferences can be held.

Don't delay in sharing information. Incorrect stories spread quickly. Never try to cover up or exaggerate a situation. Avoid placing blame. Don't argue with reporters. Stick with the communication policy and agreed-upon statements. Share the facts. It is imperative that every effort to report the facts be made as soon as possible.

THE AFTERMATH OF A CRISIS

Mental health professionals state that school officials and administrators will need to take a long-term view of dealing with the aftermath of a crisis. Many children and adults need to talk about what they experienced. Expression of their frustrations and fears, as well as the need to understand why the event occurred, are important to the healing process. Be aware that many psychological symptoms associated with the trauma may not appear for weeks or months after the incident.

POST-TRAUMATIC STRESS

The findings of Dr. Robert Pynoos, director of UCLA's Prevention Intervention Program in Trauma, Violence and Sudden Bereavement in Childhood, provide strong evidence that acute post-traumatic stress results from violent life threats. The severity is related to the extent of exposure or the witnessing of injury or death. Stress symptoms include startled reactions to loud noises, the inability to concentrate, nightmares, guilt over survival or failure to intervene, and fear of a recurrence of the incident. Some symptoms occur whether the child was present during the incident or not. Children also complain of feeling less interest in play or other enjoyable activities and feeling more distant from parents or friends.

Young children may re-enact the incident in their play. Older children may adopt risky behaviors. Students may also avoid the area where the incident took place. Anxiety may also be triggered. For example, many parents report that after their child experienced a dangerous incident, violence on television acted as a traumatic reminder.

The Greenwood, South Carolina, elementary school incident in this chapter is an excellent example of the benefits of professional counseling for students and teachers involved in a traumatic incident.

THE GRIEF PROCESS

Studies show that children mourn much as adults do. However they experience grief somewhat differently because of their age. Disbelief, anger and pain often last for a year. Parents and teachers should be aware of the differences in order to help the children deal with their feelings.

For example, sometimes children have dreams about a deceased person that frighten them. They may interpret the dream as a sign of the return of the dead, or the appearance of a ghost. Their grief reactions may often confuse, frighten or disturb them and they won't talk about their feelings with anyone. Violent death complicates the process. Overcoming the trauma of witnessing a violent event can interfere with the grief process.

It is important for teachers in the classroom and parents at home to talk with students about death and their feelings of loss. It is important to openly acknowledge the loss and talk about the children's anger and sadness.

Worrying About Others

Many children feel extreme stress about the safety of their parents, siblings or friends during a violent incident.

They may become irritable, reject those who are trying to help, and distance themselves from teachers and family. Parents should reassure children about the safety of the family and be supportive when worries intensify. Children should be encouraged to talk about their feelings.

Setting Up Counseling Centers

Schools should take certain steps before, during, and after an emergency situation. They should:

- Determine what mental health resources will be available.
- Know which community and district mental health professionals to call.
- Offer grief counseling training.
- Keep the school open for counseling and information the day of any incident and several days afterward.
- Offer counseling services for weeks and months after any incident.

After the Cleveland Elementary shooting in Stockton, California, for example, the school opened a counseling center for parents in a nearby church and set up a 24-hour hotline to take calls from families dealing with the after-effects of the tragedy.

Post-traumatic stress symptoms can last for as long as two years after a crisis. Cleveland Elementary principal Busher said, "I find that people who are removed from the situation sometimes have a real lack of understanding. They feel that the incident is over, so why are people not going on about their lives, business as usual? That's really not possible."

Anniversaries of the event or other crises around the country can trigger a renewal of symptoms.

Counseling should be offered to school staff and officials as well as to parents and children. Children often observe their teachers carefully in response to an event and this makes staff recovery doubly important. Counseling for recovery is necessary for teachers and staff in terms of their own welfare and that of the students.

After a Crisis

School should reopen after the day a crisis occurs if possible. All traces of violence should be cleaned up by maintenance personnel and children should be reassured that the school is a place of safety. Paying attention to physical details will help children cope with the trauma. Naturally, the perception of school as a safe place depends on what the perception was prior to any violent incident.

CONTROLLING GUNS AND PREVENTING SCHOOL VIOLENCE

RECOMMENDATIONS

There are actions that school authorities, local, state and federal governments, and the public can take to change the violent situation facing our K-12 school systems. The following recommendations, endorsed by the authors, are based on a presentation made to Congress on "Weapons in Schools" by Ronald D. Stephens, Executive Director of National School Safety Center on October 1, 1992. Some of the recommendations have been summarized to be more concise. They are:

1. Enact a comprehensive and systematic federal safe schools initiative that includes but is not necessarily limited to mandated school crime reporting, mandated safe school planning which incorporates a comprehensive student behavior management plan, age-appropriate curriculua to foster responsible citizenship among youth, and a parent and community leadership plan. Each state should establish state and regional safe school centers to help train and support youth-serving professionals and the children they serve.

2. Strengthen laws to keep guns out of the hands of criminals. More careful screening and background checks of individuals purchasing firearms should be implemented. Encourage the passage of parental responsibility laws requiring gun owners and parents to keep their weapons secured from minors. (The authors prefer to work for the passage of national legislation or state legislation if not possible at the federal level, to ban the sale or possession of all hand guns, semi-automatic or automatic weapons.)

3. Modify the Gun-Free School Zone Law to the **Weapon-Free** School Zone Law and require that each state establish clear reasonable sanctions for juveniles who transport or use a weapon in school or the community.

4. Encourage schools to adopt model weapons intervention and prevention programs, such as the STAR Program developed by the Center to Prevent Handgun Violence.

5. Develop School Safety Plans. Each school and each school district should be required to develop and implement a comprehensive and systematic safe schools plan that focuses on supervision, education and administrative leadership strategies. Designing safer schools should become part of the safe schools plan. National standards for the construction of new schools should be established to promote safety and supervision and to minimize criminal opportunities. (The National School Safety Center provides training and technical assistance in this area and has developed guidelines to assist school administrators and community leaders in developing such plans.)

6. Mandate School Crime Reporting. The Student Right to Know and Campus Security Act of 1990 passed by Congress and signed by the President requires colleges and universities, but not K-12 schools, to collect and maintain campus crime data. This is unusual because the victimization incidents are significantly higher on K-12

campuses in terms of real numbers and victimization rates. College and university students have a choice as to whether or not to attend a school. Most K-12 students are compelled to attend school and further compelled to attend a school not of their choosing.

7. Redesign Teacher Training Components. Sixty-two percent of U.S. teachers have stated that their college education did not adequately prepare them for the classroom. These programs must focus on effective classroom management, dealing with disruptive students, how to break up a fight and conflict prevention and resolution. A national panel of education experts should be appointed to develop significant and essential training standards and criteria for successful teaching.

8. Focus on Multicultural Training. By the year 2000, nearly one-third of American young people entering schools will be from minority groups. Many of the gang problems and campus violence we experience today are due to cultural and behavioral misunderstanding and intolerance. Training is needed to better understand, appreciate and accept the ethnic and cultural diversity in our nation's schools. Teacher training institutions and our public schools should be encouraged to adopt such programs. Multicultural understanding and appreciation should be placed on the national agenda.

Congress or state legislatures should commission a national initiative to develop model programs and strategies that respond to these needs.

9. Implement Conflict Resolution Training/Non-Violence Curricula for Students. School violence is merely the tangible expression of conflict among students and teachers. Schoolyard bullying and intimidation is perhaps the most underrated and yet enduring problem in our schools. Half of schoolyard bullies grow up to become criminals; 25 percent become serious career criminals. We can iden-

tify these youngsters as early as kindergarten or first grade, but we tend to do little for them. If we can pursue non-violent alternatives to resolving conflicts, a significant amount of school crime can be prevented. Non-violence curricula, problem solving, goal setting, peer helping, peer mediation programs, and simple courtesy should be a part of every school's educational strategy to reduce crime and violence. In recent years, we have evaluated primarily the academic side of the report card — reading, arithmetic, and science; we have ignored the behavior side. It's time to emphasize responsible behavior.

10. Intensify Supervision and Provide Vibrant Extracurricular Programs. Supervision techniques and processes that preclude metal detectors should be considered. Youngsters need adults who are interested in them and their success. Intensified supervision programs may include a professionally trained school peace officer; parent volunteers to help supervise hallways, playgrounds, gathering areas, and other potential trouble spots; a "surrogate somebody" to serve as a role model and mentor to each child; a vivacious athletic and extracurricular program; recreation and community service opportunities.

11. Encourage Parent Participation and Parent Education Programs. "Many parents drop their kids off in kindergarten and pick them up in the 12th grade and wonder what went wrong in between." Schools and businesses need to foster and encourage more effective means for parent participation on school campuses. Site visitation, supervision, and specialty instruction are important ways for parents to become involved.

12. Establish regional and statewide School Safety Centers. Such centers could provide statewide leadership, model programs, demonstration projects and resources to school systems within their region.

13. Provide Gang/Drug Prevention and Gang Intervention Training. The gang/drug phenomena has perhaps affected education in the 1990s more than any other single issue. Gangs, drugs and weapons in school are all closely related. Gangs are on the move — and they are coming to a community near you. School administrators, law enforcers and youth-serving professionals need training in gang identification as well as in prevention and intervention strategies for combating gangs and drugs.

14. Focus on Crisis Prevention and Management. There are two kinds of school administrators — "those who have faced a crisis and those who are about to." Specialty training for administrators in crisis prevention, crisis preparation, crisis management, and crisis resolution is essential.

15. Mobilize Communities for Safer Schools. School administrators cannot solve the school crime problem alone. They need support in establishing, fostering, and developing interagency partnerships within their communities.

CHAPTER 2

BULLYING IN SCHOOLS

School bullying has grown into a serious problem not only in the United States, but also in Europe and Japan. Bullying disrupts the learning environment and causes fear among victims and potential victims. The National Association of Elementary School Principals indicates in "Report to Parents" that one in 10 students is harassed or attacked by bullies and that 15 percent of all school children are involved in bully/victim problems.

According to Dr. Dan Olweus, a Professor who specializes in victimization research, at the University of Bergen in Norway, American schools harbor approximately 2.1 million bullies and 2.7 million of their victims. Three percent of students in first through ninth grades are bullied about once a week or more. While most educators are aware of bullying, most of the confrontations are dismissed as the unpleasant inevitabilities of growing up. Dr. Nathaniel Floyd, a clinical psychologist for the Board of Cooperative Educational Services in New York, says that bullies are everywhere. They don't stop just because graduation comes. If not stopped, bullies will go on to bully people in business and in interpersonal relationships. It becomes a way of life. Many bullying incidents have tragic endings.

DeKalb, Missouri

Consider the following example in a rural high school in Missouri.

Classes at a rural high school, DeKalb High in Missouri, had just begun on a Monday in March 1987, when Nathan D. Faris, a 12-year-old who had been taunted as "Chubby," pulled a pistol from a duffel bag and shot his classmate, Timothy Perrin, age 13, of Tushville, in the head. Seventh grade students ran from the social studies classroom seeking safety while Nathan then shot himself in the head. Students later told highway patrol trooper Bob Anderson that Nathan had been the object of relentless teasing. Classmates referred to him as a "walking dictionary" and called him fat. "It's been happening ever since the third or fourth grade," said classmate Benji Chapman, age 12. "People teased him because he wore sunglasses. They called him *Sunny*— and because he's fat."

Students explained that when Nathan first pulled out the gun, others began to taunt him, doubting that the weapon was real. Tim jumped up and grabbed Nathan's wrists trying to get him to let go. Apparently Tim thought it was a fake gun. He let go and went back to his seat laughing. Nathan then fired a shot at Tim but missed. Students gasped and some ran as Nathan fired more shots. Tim was wounded by one of the shots and staggered out of the room. Nathan then turned the gun on himself. Tim survived his wounds but Nathan was not so fortunate.

HARASSMENT OF GIRLS

According to one survey, bullying in the form of sexual harassment of girls is rampant in U.S. schools, ranging from written notes to attempted rape. Nan Stein, director of Wellesley College's Center for Research on Women in

Boston and leading researcher of the survey, says, "There are assaults going on right in front of adults' eyes and the adults aren't intervening." While this survey was not considered a scientific study due to a lack of randomly selected respondents, the findings matched parents' complaints, reports from school administrators, and lawsuits. The survey of 2,000 people included girls ranging from ten to eighteen years old. Eighty-nine percent of the female students in this age group reported being the subject of sexual comments, gestures, and looks. Eighty-three percent said they had been pinched, touched or grabbed. The reported harassment almost always involved fellow students, but four percent said they had been harassed by teachers, administrators or other school staff. In two-thirds of the incidents, other people witnessed the harassment but in over half the cases, teachers or administrators took no action.

ADDRESSING THE BULLYING PROBLEM

The National School Safety Center sponsored an international gathering of education authorities in 1987. The practicum participants introduced five central ideas to be acknowledged by the public and school administrators to help solve the problem of bullying. These ideas are:

1. Educators should recognize that school bullying is a significant problem.

2. Educators should recognize that fear and suffering are becoming part of the everyday lives of victims of bullying, causing them to avoid certain areas at school, stay home from school, run away, and in isolated cases, commit suicide.

3. Educators and parents should realize that young bullies are likely to become criminals in adulthood and to suffer from family and professional problems. Early prevention can not only stop bullying, but also can save vic-

tims, the bully, and society from years of potentially tragic problems.

4. Educators and society should discard the idea that fights among children are normal youthful aggressive behavior.

5. The United States should follow the lead of Norway, Sweden, and Japan, who have developed national intervention and prevention programs to address the problem.

WHAT IS A BULLY?

Bullies are quick to start a fight. The use of force, belligerence, and intimidation are the means they most often use. They are overly aggressive, destructive, and enjoy dominating other children. This is why they stand out from the normal active and assertive play of childhood. They are children who have learned that aggressive behaviors such as kicking, hitting, and biting offer rewarding results. Bullies also shout insults, make threats, and call names. Vanderbilt University psychologist Dr. Kenneth Dodge's research shows that by the age of seven or eight, bullies already are in the habit of misinterpreting an innocent brush or bump as a blatant attack. "Bullies see the world with a paranoid's eye and feel justified in retaliating for what actually are imaginary harms."

Research shows that bullies don't realize how aggressive they are. Dr. Robert Selman, psychologist and Associate Professor at Harvard's Graduate School of Education and School of Medicine, believes that the anger and aggressive behavior bullies express are caused by immature thinking patterns. Human thinking may be categorized into three levels, progressing from a primitive, commanding attitude to a heightened ability to collaborate and cooperate with others. These levels are:

1. Unilateral-one way commands and assertions of one's own needs

2. Self-reflective/reciprocal — a focus on verbal persuasion, convincing others, making deals, or using other methods that protect one's own interest in any negotiating process and

3. Collaborative — a more sophisticated level when one understands that a relationship's continuity is more important than the particular issue at hand.

Bullies fall into the unilateral thinking level or worse.

Research also shows that boy bullies are three to four times more likely to inflict physical assaults than girls. But girls tend to be more psychologically manipulative and subtle, shunning their victims or ostracizing them in other ways. While boy bullies suffer serious lifelong problems if there is no intervention in their behavior, more aggressive girls grow into mothers who punish their children harshly.

WHEN BULLIES GROW UP

A class bully who terrorizes his peers on the school playground has a one in four chance of having a criminal record by the age of thirty according to a 22-year study in this area. Other children have about a one in 20 chance of becoming a criminal. Leonard Eron, and other psychologists at the University of Illinois-Chicago, traced 870 third-graders from Columbia County, New York, by analyzing factors such as how punitive the parents were, whether they rejected their children, and the amount of violence the children saw on television.

Researchers followed more than 400 of their original subjects since 1960. The children who were the most aggressive as youngsters were also the most likely to drop out of school and were in trouble with the law as teenagers. Of the 409 children who were found at age 30, those who had been childhood bullies tended to have children who were bullies. The men were also found to be abusive toward their wives, to punish their children severely, and to have been convicted for violent crimes.

What does this mean in our schools? "Once this pattern is set and time goes on, it becomes harder and harder for kids to change," says Dr. Eron. Often, bullying behavior increases and manifests itself on college campuses in violent behavior such as hazing and other alcohol related incidents that take place in fraternities and sororities. All researchers agree that early intervention by caring and attentive adults is crucial.

The researchers found that the three ideal conditions for learning aggression are: seeing examples of it, including television; being rewarded for acting in that fashion, and being an object of aggression.

Evidence strongly suggests that bullying tends to be an inter-generational problem. Many childhood bullies were abused at home by a parent and witnessed parental spousal abuse or abuse of their siblings. Living with abusive parents teaches children that aggression and violence are effective and appropriate means to attain a goal.

Studies show that parents of bullies tend to ignore their children and go to extremes in discipline. Dr. Ronald Slaby, a Harvard psychologist who has studied bullies, says parents often wrongly teach their children to strike back at the least provocation. "Perhaps our schools and our culture have been remiss in teaching how to be assertive without being aggressive, and by assertive I mean standing up for one's rights, holding one's ground, without being hostile," he says.

Young children also learn to dominate others through watching violent television programs. Studies suggest that after watching aggression on television, children see such behavior as a successful form of social interaction and act more aggressively with their peers.

The authors of *Social Development in Young Children* note that there is no evidence supporting the commonly held view that watching aggression enables children to release "pent-up hostility" that otherwise might result in aggressive behavior. To the contrary, viewing aggressive incidents increases children's knowledge of how to perform aggressive acts and reduces their inhibitions against behaving aggressively themselves.

WHO ARE THE VICTIMS?

In general, victims are physically weaker than other boys or girls, while bullies are stronger and bigger than average. Victims of bullying are not always that different from other kids. Being overweight, wearing glasses or having some other unusual characteristics does not necessarily invite victimization.

Most adults will not tolerate bullying and will get support from some source if necessary. Children do not have the same recourse. They suffer from more than the obvious bruises and scrapes inflicted. A child who is bullied may be stigmatized by other children as well, eroding their self confidence. An attitude of self reproach is often assumed by victims. They may feel they deserve the taunting, teasing or other harassment. They may withdraw and take less part in social and intellectual situations. They are often overprotected by parents who encourage dependent behavior. Other victims, like their attackers, may be victims of abuse in their own home.

BULLYING IN JAPAN

Bullying is considered a major problem in Japan where violence, general delinquency, and vandalism are increasing. The Japanese government called for major education reform due to extensive bullying. Dr. Gerald Lesser, a Harvard Professor of Education who has researched the problems in Japan, says "Bullies are receiving a lot of attention in Japan because they're not consistent with the behavioral norm of Japanese culture, which teaches treating each other with courtesy and kindness." Many victims have taken their own lives as in the case of Nathan Faris.

Conversely, some victims have tried to kill their tormentors as did the young man from Kyushu, Japan.

Tokyo

In spite of his parents repeated complaints to school officials, seven-year-old Gaku Fujimoto lost his sight in his left eye after 18 months of brutality and bullying from classmates. He even hinted at suicide in his diary entries, in one of which he begged, "Please look at the many injuries on my hands and feet. Teacher, please help me quickly. I will be safe every day if I die." Nightmares tormented him. But his teacher told him to endure it — *Gaman* in the Japanese language.

Yamagata

On January 13, 1993, the body of thirteen-year-old Yuhei Kodama was found stuffed into a rolled gymnasium mat at a junior high school in Yamagata, Japan. His face was swollen to twice its normal size. The child of a well-to-do family, Yuhei had been tormented for months. His Tokyo accent made him stand out in Yamagata in northern Japan. He was beaten by seven classmates while at least twenty other pupils watched. No one reported the beating to the authorities.

Tokyo

Ryo Tsuchiya, fourteen years old, was abused emotionally, rather than physically by her friends. They would deny her existence by saying she had died and was a ghost they couldn't see. They also ordered her to carry their bags. Encouraged by her psychiatrist father, she published *The Bullied's Diary*, the first detailed account of a typical pattern of torment. The diary ignited public interest, but the school refused to comment on the problem.

While the teachers' union advocates an education program to teach tolerance of Japan's outcasts, minorities and women, they acknowledge that few teachers have time to teach it because of other standardized exam pressures and the required curriculum.

Kyushu

Another case shows the tragic price of not being able to speak out. A 20-year-old Kyushu man had been beaten by bullies every day. They tore off his clothes and even forced him to take them all off on occasions when he was in junior high school. He carried out his rage by placing arsenic in 21 bottles of beer and crafting homemade bombs for his class reunion. Fortunately for the bullies, his plan was prevented from being carried out, and he was caught and sentenced to six years in prison.

Addressing the Problem - Japan

Academic pressure and isolation are strong in Japan's group society which tends to create a different type of bully. Cases involve several youngsters ganging up on one child. The phenomenon is made worse by the declining Japanese family, from the three-generation households of the past to the current one-generation family with an average of fewer than two children.

While the number of violent crimes reported to the Ministry of Education dropped from a peak of 155,066 in 1985 to 22,062 in 1991, there are still complaints from people who say the bullying problem is ignored by school officials. To prevent bullying the teachers union is advocating a human rights education program to teach tolerance. One Tokyo high school, Higashi Kurume Junior High, has curbed the problem by developing strict student/teacher rules to curb the growing incident of violence against teachers. The principal abolished all rules imposed from the top and allowed students to make their own rules in consultation with teachers. The more democratic environment led to a significant decrease in cases of bullying.

The Japanese Ministry of Health and Welfare, in response to the problems of bullying and violence, has appointed 14,000 child-welfare workers to help deal with bullying and child abuse.

SCHOOL LIABILITY PROBLEMS

In addition to the problems of physical and mental injury, schools face significant exposure to liability when bullying occurs. Parents of a ten-year-old boy filed a lawsuit for $351,000 against the San Francisco School District for failing to enforce the child's right to attend a safe, secure and peaceful school. In Japan, one family filed a 22 million yen damage suit against the Tokyo Metropolitan Government and parents of two alleged bullies, claiming their thirteen-year-old son's suicide was caused by the bullying.

School attendance and the overall campus climate of safety is affected by bullying. Victims fear school and the abuse that awaits them there. Twenty-five percent of students surveyed in a 1984 study by the National Association of Secondary School Principals said that one of their most serious concerns was fear of bullies.

BULLYING IN NORWAY AND SWEDEN

Dr. Dan Olweus found in his studies that over 15 percent of schoolchildren are involved in bully-victim problems. One in 10 students is regularly attacked or harassed by bullies. These figures are based on surveys of more than 150,000 elementary and junior high school students in Norway and Sweden. Dr. Olweus believes the statistics are representative of the United States as well. Schoolyard bullying is a significant and pervasive problem. Current research replicating Dr. Olweus' study is being conducted at Florida Atlantic University in the United States.

METHODS OF INTERVENTION

Dr. Olweus found that traditional methods of treatment for bullies such as psychodrama, psychoanalysis, and group therapy have been of little value. He established an experimental intervention program in 42 schools at the request of the government and results indicate that bullying incidents were cut by more than half in the program's first two years. After working in the United States at Stanford University, Dr. Olweus published his findings and recommended an action program that would apply in the U.S. Among his recommendations are:

- Insure that there is adult supervision at recess.
- Practice strict enforcement of straightforward rules of behavior.
- Mete out consistent, non-physical punishment to misbehaving children.
- Help bullying victims to assert themselves and make them valuable in the eyes of the class.
- Parents should encourage their children to develop and maintain new friendships.
- Both parents and teachers must encourage better communication.
- There must be a clear repudiation of repeated physical and mental maltreatment.

SCHOOL INTERVENTION

Programs that deal with school bullying are in place in several school districts in the United States. Dr. Nathanial Floyd started an anti-bullying program in Southern Westchester County, New York. Chronic bullies are counseled individually and in groups. Incentives to cooperate with peers and encouragement to gain control over the need to bully, partly by assessing their views of potential victims as vulnerable, are given. The most effective strategy for victims when confronting bullies, according to Dr. Floyd, is to make a stand with dignity, rather than to fight aggressively. Victims are taught assertiveness in role playing, counseling, and group discussions.

At English High School in Boston, bullies are warned before suspension. Then they are counseled by doctoral candidates in psychology from Harvard University who monitor their progress. School system psychologists are called in for serious cases.

BULLYING PREVENTION PLAN

A strategy for preventing or controlling bullying in schools should include the following:

1. Assess the problem through a questionnaire to teachers and students.

2. Communicate clear and consistent behavior standards.

3. Closely monitor playground activity — Be visible on campus.

4. Establish intervention programs. Warn or suspend offenders. Serious cases should be referred to school psychologists.

5. Provide group and individual counseling for chronic bullies. Offer incentives to cooperate with peers and encouragement to gain control over the need to bully.

RECOMMENDED ACTIONS FOR VICTIMS OF BULLYING

Victims should be taught to make a stand and leave the field with dignity, not necessarily to prevent a bully's potential to fight. Assertiveness should be taught through group discussions, role playing, and counseling. Checklists should be made available for teachers to help them identify potential bullies and victims and steer them to help. Dr. Floyd, clinical psychologist, Board of Cooperative Educational Services, New York, believes current trends in today's society to sue, criticize, and blame are partially responsible for the bullying phenomenon. "Kids are influenced by the culture, which endorses belittling and teasing, especially at athletic competitions. In truth, we have become a blaming society," he says.

Parents' Guide to Identifying Bullying

1. Be aware that bullying is a serious problem.

2. Be aware that victims are physically weaker, often younger.

3. Recognize this is a real problem for children.

4. Immediately inform your child's school of your concerns if incidents take place at school, en route or elsewhere.

5. Watch for symptoms. Victims may experience a drop in grades, be hesitant to go to school, become withdrawn, come home with torn clothes and unexplained bruises. Be suspicious if a child needs extra supplies or lunch money, a bully may be extorting money. If your child takes toys or others possessions to schools and regularly loses them, find out why.

6. Talk and listen to your child. Encourage children to share information about school, social events, the ride to and from school. Openly communicate — without prying. Listen to their conversation with other children also.

7. Don't bully your child yourself. Examine your family's discipline measures. Try to teach children to obey rules by non-physical, consistently enforced means.

8. Teach your child to be independent. Rather than tell your child to fight back or ignore bullies, teach them to stand up for themselves verbally. Expose them to programs that boost self esteem. Encourage them to develop friendships. A resourceful, confident child with friends is less likely to be bullied.

A 90-page book published by NSSC, *Set Straight On Bullies* provides a comprehensive examination of the bully-victim problem. "School Bullying and Victimization," an NSSC Resource Paper, is also a good resource. See the Resource Section for NSSC's address.

CHAPTER 3

VIOLENCE IN COLLEGES AND UNIVERSITIES

NATIONWIDE COLLEGE VIOLENCE

University of Georgia

While asleep in her bed on January 17, 1988, Dana Getzinger was awakened suddenly by a pillow thrust over her face. During the struggle Dana thought her attacker, a man with a ski mask and gloves who had slipped through a sliding glass door and passed three sleeping roommates, delivered a sharp blow to her stomach. It was actually a knife and it punctured her lower aorta and liver. She kicked her attacker and managed to get to her feet. Dana instinctively grabbed the blade with her hands to avoid another stabbing. Amidst her screams for help, the masked intruder ran. Only Dana's strength as a former gymnast and her cardiovascular reserve as a runner probably saved her life. Her descending aorta had been punctured and two cardiovascular surgeries were required.

Investigation revealed that Dana's apartment complex was a literal hunting ground for crime, and students were the targets. Many thefts occurred regularly in the area.

After the attack, both Dana and her parents realized the tremendous lack of "student/parent" awareness of campus crime. No suspect was apprehended and nothing more was learned about the attacker.

University of Rochester

On January 20, 1987, at Susan B. Anthony Residence Hall, University of Rochester, senior Darrell Tornay, 20 was stabbed by UR freshman William Griffin, age 18. Griffin had a blood alcohol level of .25, two and a half times the legal limit for driving, on the night of the stabbing. Two other students were stabbed. Darrell Tornay died a month later from an infection beneath the liver following complicated surgery. The death was ruled a homicide.

Simon's Rock College

In December of 1992, Wayne Lo, an 18-year-old honor student and violin virtuoso shot and killed two people and injured four others in a murderous rampage. Police spokesmen said Lo lugged a modified AK-47 assault rifle through the snowy Berkshire mountains campus at Great Barrington, Massachusetts, and opened fire, killing Spanish Professor Nacanan Saez and Galen Gibson, an 18-year-old student from Gloucester, Massachusetts. Four other students were injured but survived.

University of California

A gang of teens called "pack rats" by police, in 1987 followed three UC Berkeley students to their dormitory and after exchanging words, smashed the face of a female student with a brick, causing severe injuries which required plastic surgery.

Bethune Cookman College

In February, 1993, three undergraduate students of Bethune Cookman College in Daytona Beach, Florida, were shot to death and a fourth injured as they sat in their car on the edge of the college campus. The students were ambushed by four men who told police they thought the students were men they had fought with at a local restaurant.

Santa Fe Community College

Elizabeth Foster, a 21-year-old student at Santa Fe Community College in Gainesville, New Jersey, disappeared on March 15, 1992. Last seen on campus, her nude body was discovered on March 16, 1992 in the woods near a restaurant where her car was found. Investigators said she had been severely beaten. Foster was the eighth student killed in two years in Gainsville. A suspect in five of the killings was taken into custody.

Lehigh University

In April of 1986, Jeanne Ann Clery, a freshman student at Lehigh University in Pennsylvania was raped and killed in her dormitory room by a fellow student who didn't know her. Jeanne Clery's assailant attacked her while she was sleeping in her bed. Joseph Henry had entered the dormitory through three doors propped open by students. Henry was taken into custody within two days and arrested for the murder of Jeanne Clery.

After a lengthy trial, Joseph Henry was convicted of Murder One by the jury and sentenced to death.

The parents of Jeanne, Connie and Howard Clery, became so concerned over the negative attitude toward safety and security and unreported violence on campus by the officials of Lehigh University that they sued the University for negligence, failure to protect, and to warn.

SECURITY ON CAMPUS, INC.

In 1987, after the murder trial of Jeanne's killer was over and the civil suit versus Lehigh University was settled out of court, the Clerys decided to form an organization to prevent the tragedy of similar murders from happening at other colleges. They founded Security On Campus, Inc. which set in motion a train of events to do the following:

- Uncover the previously well-kept secret of campus crime.

- Provide student victims and their parents with emotional support and legal research for redress.

- Revolutionize and pressure colleges and universities to provide "real-world" security procedures and policies.

- Obtain federal and state laws designed to enhance the three above points and to reduce the national epidemic of violent campus crime and student alcohol and drug abuse.

Security on Campus, Inc. initiated a national media campaign to alert the country about the scandal of college campus crime. Surveys by USA Today, The Santa Monica Rape Crisis Center, and Towson State University's Study for the Prevention of Campus Violence revealed the depths of the national scandal. They found the following:

- Every week, nationally, a student is murdered on a college campus or adjacent to campus.

- One out of six students will be raped or sexually assaulted during their academic careers. Rape of male students is a growing occurrence.

- Over 30 percent of students will be victims of felonies, i.e. murder, rape, robbery, aggravated assault and arson.

- Eighty percent of student felonies are committed by students on students.

- Felonies, per hundred students, on a national basis are virtually the same for urban, suburban and rural campuses.

- Administrators at far too many campuses do not enforce state under-age drinking laws and federal narcotics laws.

- Between 70 and 80 percent of student felons who commit crimes are alcohol and drug abusers.

SOC, Inc., also prepared and mailed free of charge over three hundred thousand Campus Security Questionnaires to students and their parents. A copy of the questionnaire is located in Appendix II. They initiated and obtained passage of Campus Security and Crime Reporting laws, to date, in eighteen states and obtained passage of three strong federal laws — The Student Right to Know and Campus Security Act of 1990, the Campus Sexual Assault Victims Bill of Rights Act of 1992, and the clarification of the Buckley Amendment to the Family Educational Rights and Privacy Act (F.E.R.P.A.). President George Bush signed these acts into law in 1992.

These laws mandate that schools receiving federal funding report crime rates to federal authorities, that colleges notify sexual assault victims of their rights, provide services to victims, and establish policies concerning sexual assault, and enforce all state under-age drinking laws and federal narcotic laws. The campuses must report all campus felony statistics to the Secretary of Education annually, to students, faculty and staff, and upon request to prospective students and their parents on a timely basis during the course of the academic year. The Campus Sexual Assault Victims Act also requires that campus administrators treat student victims with dignity, secure evidence, provide justice, and immediate medical and psychological aid and reveal to victims the disciplinary action given to the perpetrators.

Senators and Representatives were amazed that the grass roots campaign got a law passed in only eight months, but they didn't know the intensity of Howard and Connie

Clery's efforts. Lobbyists for the colleges and universities fought hard to kill the bill in committees and then tried to gut it with self-serving amendments when the law passed without opposition in Congress.

LETTERS TO SECURITY ON CAMPUS

It is not difficult to understand the success of Security on Campus when you consider the support of other families of victims. Following is one of the many poignant letters received by SOC.

Dear SOC:

It was early August, 1984. I stood in the waiting room at La Guardia airport and waved to my daughter, Karin, as she boarded the plane to New Orleans with no idea that I would never see her again. A year earlier, at the start of her freshman year at Tulane, I had boarded the plane with her and later taken the airport cab to her school. I wanted to see her safely settled in her dormitory room. Somehow, that second year I forgot all that. Because of her low standing in the housing lottery, common in second year students, she was living off-campus. We never questioned the security arrangements - after all, it was scarcely a block and a half from her first year dorm. We never asked about bars on windows, locks on doors, neighbors.

October 26, 1984 would have been a special day. My wife, Arlene, and I had plane tickets to visit Karin in New Orleans on her 19th birthday, see her new apartment and take in the World's Fair — all in one long weekend. October 26th never happened. Instead, our life stopped at 8:15 p.m. on October 3rd with a call from the Medical Examiner in New Orleans. Our daughter had been found in her apartment, bound and strangled, with the alarm clock for her morning classes still buzzing.

Today, I'm left with a bedroom I can hardly bear to enter, picture albums I can't look at, home movies I'll never be able to see — and no daughter.

Where are my feelings today? A tremendous sense of both loss and guilt. At that time we never thought to ask about crime rates at college campuses, about off-campus housing, about crime rates in the community surrounding the college.

How stupid we were! But how different our college decision might have been if those figures had been provided to us by colleges and guidance counselors even if I was too dumb to ask!

Letter written April 1989 by Karin's parents.

Dr. & Mrs. Wilfred Minkin
Armonk, New York

HOW BAD IS THE VIOLENCE ON CAMPUSES?

More than 7,500 cases of violent crimes in college campuses were reported in the first crime reports listed under the Campus Security Act. Included in those 1991 crimes are 30 murders, 1,000 rapes, and more than 1,800 robberies. Property violations included 8,981 motor vehicle thefts and 32,127 burglaries. These statistics were reported by 2,400 colleges as required by the federal government. Constance Clery of Security on Campus, Inc., still believes colleges are not divulging all their crime information. "Our only opposition in the whole crusade was from colleges themselves, attempting to keep campus crime undercover," she says.

COLLEGE AND UNIVERSITY HAZING

Hazing has been and is a problem on university campuses across the country. Violence in the form of mental and physical abuse is condoned and continues today through the initiation rites for fraternities and sororities.

The Greek System (fraternities and sororities) in particular continues to be plagued. Many fraternity pledges are injured and killed in pledge hazing rites every year. The use and abuse of alcohol by persons of legal and illegal age, and the unacceptable conduct growing out of such use, are major elements of the problem. Alcohol consumption has been identified as a central ingredient of many of the antisocial incidents which have occurred, including fights, acquaintance rapes, resistance to law enforcement personnel, destruction of property, and a general disregard for the rights and privileges of others.

HOW DANGEROUS IS HAZING?

An estimated 20 students have been killed in hazing and other fraternity activities and rites from 1983 to 1993 and many more injured. Another 29 pledges were killed in the previous decade according to Hank Nuwer, author of the book *Broken Pledges* (Longstreet Press, Inc. 1990). Eileen Stevens of the Committee to Halt Useless College Killings (C.H.U.C.K.), and others interested in the hazing problem, believe the number of deaths and injuries from hazing are significantly higher. Many of the causes of hazing deaths and injuries are covered up and classified as an accident. Secrecy shrouds the practice. This is done to protect the organization from officials for unauthorized fraternity activities. Hazing incidents occur across the country and not only in fraternities. Even sororities abuse their pledges. Summarized below are a few of the many hazing injuries and incidents that have occurred in the last couple of years.

Southern University, LA

A 23-year-old student was hit on the head with a frying pan during an initiation rites and blinded. It was doubtful that he would regain his sight.

Auburn University, Auburn, AL

University administrators put the honor society, Spades, on probation for mental hazing. Fraternity members tied a student pledge to a tree and told him that he was to be killed.

University of North Texas, Denton, TX

A 20-year-old student, Michael Brown, was hospitalized for acute alcohol poisoning that reached a level of .42, more than four times the amount at which a person is considered legally drunk in Texas. Three members of the Pi Kappa Alpha fraternity were arrested by the police.

Clark Atlanta University, Atlanta, GA

During an initiation at the Omega Psi Phi fraternity, pledge Roderick Green, 21, was brutally paddled by members so badly that he was hospitalized with an injured kidney. Another student at the Phi Beta Sigma fraternity was hospitalized also with severe kidney damage after being paddled by members.

Rutgers University, New Brunswick, NJ

The Delta Upsilon fraternity was banned for three years after being cited for offenses including branding the buttocks of pledges and requiring them to perform a variety of tasks for members.

Indiana University, Bloomington, IN

Dennis Jay, 21, a pledge of Alpha Tau Omega, was allegedly forced to drink a bottle of wine, a fifth of whiskey, and another half of a fifth of whiskey in a hazing incident. He was one of 20 pledges being initiated. They were stripped to their underwear, blindfolded, and led around the fraternity house. Sorority girls tugged at their shorts and wrote on their bodies with Magic Markers. They were forced to drink from "beer bongs," containers with a funnel and plastic tube.

Jay collapsed from drinking so much and was taken to a hospital. Fortunately his life was saved even though his alcohol content reached 0.48 (.50 is considered a fatal amount). It took him seven hours to regain consciousness. When Jay woke up in the Bloomington Hospital he had tubes in his nose, needles in his arms and a ventilator hose down his throat. His response, "Man, I must have drunk a lot. This is gonna be trouble." He was right.

Some of the fraternity brothers asked Jay not to tell official or authorities about the hazing. Fraternity pledges are asked to take vows of silence. Later he heard that fraternity members were telling investigators that Jay was an alcoholic loser who had stumbled into the frat house in need of medical help. Often victims of hazing are blamed for what happened. That made Jay angry. He told authorities what had actually happened. The university expelled the chapter for their hazing activities.

Dennis Jay transferred to Holy Cross College in South Bend, Indiana, but did not join a fraternity. Later when **People Magazine** asked Jay about his attitude on fraternities, he said, "What kind of system forces people to run around naked, behave like morons and drink too much? It's the most immature thing in the world."

University of Texas, Austin, TX

Some members of the Sigma Nu fraternity decided that one of the pledges needed special treatment. After beating him they used a claw hammer to lead him around by his genitals to humiliate him. The university suspended Sigma Nu for six years. Three of the fraternity brothers were prosecuted and fined $500 and court costs.

Gallaudet University (School for the deaf), Washington, DC

You would think that deaf students have enough problems without becoming involved in hazing. A pledge of the

Kappa Gamma fraternity was allegedly forced to stand in a meeting room for several hours without moving. Kevin Clark finally collapsed injuring himself in the fall. He was taken unconscious to a hospital were he recovered later. The university suspended the fraternity for four years.

Kent State University, Kent, OH — Sororities Too!

Apparently some sororities play as rough as some fraternities in initiation rites. The sisters paddle pledges, subject them to sleep deprivation, force them to chant inane sayings, and pour mustard and other smelly foods on their heads. At the Alpha Kappa Alpha sorority initiation, some pledges were paddled severely, called "taking wood." Pledge Darlene Jeter was hit more than 100 times and bled profusely from her buttocks. One sorority member was prosecuted and found guilty of hazing.

FOREIGN UNIVERSITIES

Ateneo University, Manila, Philippines

After a brutal beating by members of the Aquila Legis legal fraternity, pledge Leonard Villa died. He and other pledges were paddled and their mouths were used as ashtrays. After pressure from the government, the university expelled 12 members of the fraternity.

STEMMING HAZING DEATHS AND INJURIES

Many universities and colleges have worked to stem the tide of hazing incidents by anti-hazing policies, sanctions, and education. Pressure by universities, insurance companies, and parent and victim organizations on legislators have resulted in anti-hazing laws being passed by 37 States to date. Due to claims filed from hazing accidents, universities and Greek organizations often face higher insurance premiums or cancellation of coverage. Even with laws and policies against hazing, organizations continue the practice in secret.

Authorities often don't find out that hazing is occurring until an injury or death occurs. College fraternity members are sworn to secrecy about their activities. As a result of pressure to stop hazing, the fraternities have gone underground and become even more secret about the rituals. Many officials believe that the best way to get fraternities' attention is by hitting them in the pocketbook with lawsuits that cost them money.

When student pledges protest or speak out about hazing incidents they are often threatened and come under pressure to keep quiet or be "blackballed." Todd Wilkins, a member of Lambda Chi Alpha at the University of Wisconsin, reported a fraternity hazing. He received harassing telephone calls, had his tires slashed, and was beaten by fraternity members while walking with his girlfriend. Wilkins quit the fraternity and the university as a result.

THE NATURE OF HAZING

Medical Analysis

In a letter to the Editor of the **New York Times**, February 9, 1993, two medical doctors, Mark L. Taff and Lauren R. Boglioli of West Hempstead, LI, responded to a previous article that hazing had gone underground. The two doctors had written to the medical community in 1985 that hazing was a health hazard and had medico-legal implications. They reported that 168 known hazing injuries and deaths had occurred in the United States from 1923 to 1982. The types of injuries included those from blunt force, burns, cold exposure, heat exhaustion, acute alcohol intoxication, food and laxative poisoning, gunshot, asphyxia, electrocution, cannon and beer keg explosions, and a variety of sexual and psychological torture.

As to the actual number of deaths and injuries occurring, they said, "Our data represented the tip of the iceberg because of lack of a formal reporting system and the heavy dependence on news accounts for data collection.

Health care professionals lacked an index of suspicion when treating victims of hazing for a variety of ailments."

They found that the "profile of a victim is typically a white male 19 to 20 years old who comes to a health care facility between February and April or September and October." The majority of cases originated in college towns in the mid-Atlantic and south Atlantic States.

Their research indicates that: "Hazing is a form of group dynamics similar to cults in which individuals give up their identity and conform to the beliefs of the group. An aggressive conversion (brainwashing) is designed to break down pre-existing beliefs and replace them with new values and commitments. College fraternities subject their pledges to three stages of conversion: (1) isolation of the individual from his past life; (2) psychological abandonment from one's former self through humiliation and guilt, and (3) assumption of a new identity compatible with the fraternal organization."

The doctors reported that the fraternity system has been with us in the United States since 1850 and that hazing occurs in other groups and organizations: "Common threads exist between fraternity hazing and other organizations (religious orders, prisons, the armed services, political movements, professional organizations, and businesses) in which traditional rites of passage are required for young men to prove their manhood."

The doctors believe "The only way to eliminate hazing is to change the attitudes of society. The psychodynamics of fraternity hazing are complex, and greater efforts must be made to curb this dangerous practice."

Mayo Clinic Finding

In an article, entitled, "Hazing: Campus Rituals Can Turn Into Tragedy," in the Mayo Clinic's newsletter of September 1989, the author substantiated what the two doctors, Taff and Boglioli, found in their studies about

physical and psychological abuse of pledges. The article reported that most pledging deaths came from drowning and falls from heights, such as from a bridge or the top of a staircase. Alcohol was linked to 97 percent of all hazing injuries and deaths. Illegal drugs also were a factor.

As to psychological abuse, the article stated, "Under the best conditions, college is stressful. Hazing, with its peer pressure to conform and be accepted, can add to the tension that students face. Some hazing rituals themselves may be psychologically abusive. Examples include regiments of punishment or discipline."

The American Journal of Forensic Medicine and Pathology reported that only about 45 percent of those injured during hazing rituals received medical attention. Fear of retaliation, censure by school officials or confrontation with the law on the part of both pledges and members may be the reason.

The Mayo Clinic article ends with this comment, "Common sense and self-discipline on the part of both pledges and members, as well as consistent regulations and sanction, can help control this problem. Otherwise, needless injuries and deaths will continue to occur on our college and university campuses."

C.H.U.C.K.

Out of a terrible tragedy a new movement or organization may emerge spearheaded by a surviving mate or parent. Mothers Against Drunk Driving (MADD) and Security on Campus, Inc. were initiated after the death of a child. So was C.H.U.C.K., an acronym for the Committee to Halt Useless College Killings. It was started by Eileen Stevens after her son Chuck was killed during a Klan Alpine fraternity hazing at Alfred University, New York.

With the temperature at nine degrees Fahrenheit on the night of February 24, 1978, nine pledges, including

Chuck, were put in the trunks of three different cars — three pledges to a trunk. Chuck and the other two were given a fifth of wine, a pint of bourbon, and six-pack of beer and told that they wouldn't be released until they had consumed all of the alcohol. The fraternity's idea was that the pledges would get sick, vomit, and complete the initiation rites of the fraternity. Unfortunately, the process didn't work.

After 40 minutes the brothers opened the trunk and found Chuck and others unconscious. Instead of taking him to a hospital immediately, the members put him to bed in the fraternity house to "sleep it off." He was found dead three hours later. An autopsy showed that Chuck died of acute alcohol poisoning and exposure.

The other pledges were vomiting when taken out of the cars, but were very sick. They were taken to the hospital where two were in critical condition for 72 hours. One boy went into cardiac arrest and the other one went into a coma. Both survived the ordeal and actually became actives in the Klan Alpine fraternity.

To date the university has never acknowledged to Eileen Stevens that Chuck died in a hazing incident, nor provided her with any information resulting from an investigation of the incident. It was after this tragedy that Eileen Stevens decided to form C.H.U.C.K. to educate fraternities and sororities, university officials, parents, and legislators to eliminate all dangerous physical and mental hazing practices. The organization is not anti-fraternity, but anti-hazing. Its major goal is to bring about an awareness of hazing and prompt legislative action from states to deter hazing abuses and insure safety of students.

Starting in 1978, Eileen Stevens has lectured at over 500 campuses nationwide, spoken at numerous national fraternity conventions, and lobbied for anti-hazing laws in several states. To date, 37 states have anti-hazing laws. She has received numerous awards for her work and has been on many national talk shows and profiled by national magazines and newspapers.

CONTROL PROBLEMS FOR UNIVERSITIES

Universities operate in a limited capacity to control the affairs of fraternity and sorority chapters because those facilities are usually located off campus and privately owned and operated. Because the chapters operate off campus, but in conjunction with campus activities, university officials didn't believe they had much control. Universities are not regulators of the lives of any of their students in situations away from the campus.

However, after several disturbing incidents involving hazing and the consumption of alcohol, the University of Washington in Seattle looked into the problem and found they did have a means of control. They decided to hold fraternity and sorority chapters to high standards if they wished to associate with the university. This came about because a young woman lost the sight of one eye from an injury caused by a beer bottle thrown at a fraternity party. In keeping with this decision, they have established what is called **Individual Recognition Agreements** setting forth expectations with respect to group conduct. The agreement contains the following provisions:

1. Fraternity and sorority chapters and individual members are expected to comply with federal, state, and local laws — with emphasis on under-age drinking laws and public and fire safety regulations. They are expected to cooperate with police, fire safety officials, and representatives of the Washington State Liquor Control Board.

2. Chapters are to be held accountable for the conduct of their individual members including residents and guests.

3. Each organization must identify persons (advisers and officers) who can be contacted by police 13 hours a

day to handle any emerging problems. A list of contact people to interface with the university will also be provided.

4. Chapters must conduct uniform educational programs covering substance abuse and acquaintance rape. Additional educational programs may be required as deemed necessary.

5. Chapters must comply with the Pan Hellenic and IFC constitutions and by-laws including the Pan Hellenic Liability Management Policy which includes an explicit prohibition against the possession, sale or use of illegal drugs or controlled substances, and, among other things, a Dry Rush Policy, IFC Party Policy, Human Dignity Statement and a Dry Event Policy.

If the fraternities or sororities do not comply, they cannot take part in any university activities, essentially closing out social activities.

The Pan Hellenic Association and the Interfraternity Council (IFC), the student governing bodies of the sororities and fraternities, have adopted a number of policies to address concerns such as dry rush, a ban on open parties, and liability management. Each fraternity is required to sponsor one presentation each quarter on responsible alcohol use, date rape, and other related topics. These are a few of the policies that have emerged from student leadership in recent years. However, more are required.

HAZING PREVENTION RECOMMENDATIONS

It is recommended that colleges consider requiring that all fraternities and sorority pledges be given a "Pledge Bill of Rights" when invited into a house which states that he/she shall not be abused physically or mentally by any initiation rites. The type of abuses that pledges should not be asked to undergo are as follows:

- Sleep deprivation.

- Paddling and physical abuse.
- Forced drinking of alcohol or any alcohol drinking if under legal age.
- Physical or psychological shocks.
- Calisthenics and forced exercises.
- Any morally degrading or humiliating games or activities.
- Any intentional act on or off fraternity property or campus that causes mental or physical discomfort, excessive fatigue, embarrassment or ridicule.
- Involuntary road trips, kidnapping, or other forced activities that result in exposure to physical danger.
- Any sexual abuse of women.

Fraternity/Sorority Pledge Activities

There are hundreds of activities that pledges could take part in beside hazing type activities that would benefit the pledges, the organization, the university, and the public. For instance the pledges could do some of the following to earn their right to be a member of a house:

- Provide services to disabled groups — building ramps, etc.
- Provide services to chronically ill, frail elderly, etc., by providing transportation and doing errands.
- Visit/entertain people in institutions, hospitals.
- Assist at children day care centers.
- Assist in coaching sports at boys/girls clubs or juvenile detention facilities.
- Assist at "Food Share," "Habitat for Humanity," thrift shops for needy, etc.
- Assist at organizations providing services for people suffering from cancer, AIDS, arthritis, etc.

- Conduct studies/report on urban problems — gangs, homeless people, violence, etc.
- Sponsor programs on campus to educate students on hazing issues.
- Volunteer at a hospital, police department.
- Adopt a highway.

There is no law written in stone that says that pledges must be abused physically or mentally to prove their worth to participate in their fraternity/sorority.

FEDERAL ACTION

House Bill SHB 1082 relating to alcohol abuse and under-age drinking among college and University students was passed in February, 1993. The bill calls for colleges and universities to submit to the board and designated committees of the Legislature a comprehensive plan to combat student alcohol abuse. The plan shall include means for assuring that there is no underage drinking on campus and provide details of services that will be offered to students who are problem drinkers. In addition, the plan shall include strategies for combating underage drinking in off-campus student residences such as fraternities and sororities.

Other problems reported under the Student Right To Know Act and the Campus Sexual Assault Victims' Bill of Rights revealed other startling numbers. According to the National Victim Center:

- Over 80 percent of all sexual assaults on college campuses involve alcohol abuse.
- Twenty-two percent of all rape victims are between the ages of 18 and 24 years, or college age.

While under-age consumption of alcohol or drugs is illegal, and it is not violent in nature, violence is often the result of such consumption. The fastest growing population of rape victims is students. Four out of five of all rapes are committed by acquaintances.

Fraternities can present an environment which promulgates negative stereotypes, dangerous attitudes and abuse of alcohol and/or drugs. The result is that more gang rapes occur at fraternity chapter houses than any other college location. Acquaintance rapes occasionally occur during or after parties. In addition to sexual crimes, hazing abuses of pledging members are also prevalent as previously mentioned. Hate crimes are increasing on college campuses, from threatening telephone calls and violent personal attacks to swastikas painted on doors. Colleges attempt to assemble diverse student bodies, but when challenges to tolerance occur, violent expressions can result.

As of 1993, Security on Campus, Inc., was successful in getting five states to pass legislation called "open campus police log laws" which mandate the publication of campus police logs for public scrutiny. These laws assist victims in tracking their cases and help keep students aware of the extent of campus crime occurring on a timely basis.

The anti-hazing laws passed in thirty-seven states define activities such as hazing and make them criminal. These laws require schools to have written policies prohibiting hazing and enforcing sanctions for violating those policies. Unfortunately, enforcement is not always easy.

PUBLIC AWARENESS PROGRAM

The National Victim Center and Security on Campus, Inc. have joined in a public awareness campaign to assist college bound students and their parents. They are working in association with three other organizations: The Committee to Halt Useless College Killings (CHUCK); The Towson State University Campus Violence Prevention Center (CVPC); and the Santa Monica Medical Hospital Center's Rape Treatment Center (RTC). They provide the following material:

1. **Information Bulletins:** Overviews of campus crime issues, including a legislative report and general information on acquaintance rape and hate crimes.

2. **School Safety Checklist**: A suggestion questionnaire for students selecting a college or university. This questionnaire will help students obtain information about campus crime from the schools they are attending or are considering attending. Students and prospective students should submit this form to the Campus Police Department. High school students can ask their guidance counselors to request the information be sent to them.

3. **Safety Tips:** A specially created list of personal safety measures covering all types of violent crime on campus (this section also includes materials on acquaintance rape prevention, including recommendations for colleges to reduce the risk of rape, and an explanation of rights related to dates).

4. **What to do if You are a Victim of Crime:** Information about getting help in the unfortunate event that a student becomes a victim of crime.

COLLEGE CAMPUS SAFETY

GUIDELINES AND RECOMMENDATIONS

Summarized below are guidelines recommended for college campus students by SOC, Inc., CHUCK, CVPC, and RTC.

On the Street

- Don't walk alone after dark.
- Be alert. Look around you; be aware of who is on the street and in the area. Make it difficult for anyone to take you by surprise. (Blaring stereos, wearing

headphones, radios, etc., make you vulnerable to surprise).

- Whenever possible, it's a good idea to "dress for safety." Unlike "dressing for success," this means wearing loose fitting clothing and comfortable shoes that make walking and running easier.

- Stay on populated, well-lighted streets.

- If you think someone is following you, turn around and check; the surprise of a hostile look or aggressive word might change a potential attacker's mind. You can also head for people, lights, traffic, or run and scream. Yelling "fire" may get more results than yelling for "help."

- If a car follows you or stops, change directions; walk or run toward people, stores, or a house if necessary.

- On frequently traveled routes, note the location of emergency telephones or call boxes in public garages and parking lots *before you ever need them*.

- If you are near a public phone, call the emergency number 911 or your campus police number whenever you feel that you're in danger.

- Take self-defense classes.

Outdoors After Dark On Campus

- Always follow well-lighted paths. Stay out of shadows.

- Walk with a group whenever possible.

- Tell a friend or roommate where you are going and when you expect to return. Do not post this information on the outside of your door.

- If you must walk through the campus alone at night, call the University Police and request an escort.

- Avoid isolated places, both day and night. If you must work or study alone on weekends or holidays in offices, labs, or out-of-the-way places, lock the doors and tell a friend and the University Police where you are.

- Park your car in well-lighted areas and as close as possible to your destination.

In an Apartment or Home

- Ask local police to conduct a safety check of your home. This service is free.

- Install good locks in doors and windows. Door chains are unsafe, so use deadbolts for greater security.

- Never put personal identification tags on your key ring. Your lost key rings will be of no value to a criminal unless he/she can find the locks that your keys fit.

- Never advertise that you are not at home. Answering machine messages should never include statements like "I'm not at home now. . ."

- Likewise, never advertise that you are home alone.

- Pull shades or curtains after dark.

- If you let someone in and then have second thoughts, pretend that you are not alone.

- List last name and initials only on a mailbox, doors, in the phone book, etc.

- Don't give out information about yourself or make appointments with strangers over the phone.

- Get together with a first-time date, study partner, etc., in a public place.

- Make sure that hallways, entrances, garages, and grounds are well-lighted. Use timers or photo-sensitive devices.

- When away from home at night, or if you expect to return after dark, leave an interior light on in a room or two with the shades drawn.

- Never open the door without first checking to see who is there. Repair persons, salespeople, police, and survey takers carry identification. Ask to see it before letting them in. If someone wants to use your phone, offer to make the call while he/she waits outside.

- Leave your spare house key with a friend, not under the doormat, in a flower box, etc.

On a Date

- Acquaintance and date rape occurs more frequently on college campuses than does rape by strangers. A recent survey found that 25 percent of all female college students surveyed were victims of rape or attempted rape, and that 84 percent of those raped knew their attackers. In another survey, more than 30 percent of the male college students admitted to using force or emotional pressure to obtain sex.

- Dating individuals must communicate clearly with each other. Explicit consent should be obtained/granted before sexual activity begins. If an acquaintance or date initiates sexual activity, clearly indicate whether or not you wish this activity to continue. Give or deny consent.

In Residence Halls

- Many attacks start with casual conversation. The attacker is sizing up the situation to see how easily intimidation can be applied. If you are polite and friendly, the attacker may proceed to intimidate you.

- Although most people would recognize something strange about an encounter long before intimidation would begin, many ignore their intuition because they don't want to be unfriendly or suspicious.

- Trust your instincts. If your gut reaction to a person (stranger or acquaintance) makes you uneasy, get out of the situation as quickly as possible, even if it means being rude, making a scene, or feeling foolish.

In a Car

Park in well-lighted areas at night. Consider paying for parking. If it is essential to your safety, park wherever necessary.

- Walk to your car with your key ready.

- Check beneath the car and in the back seat before you get in to make sure that no one is hiding there.

- While driving, keep the doors locked at all times so that a person can't jump in at a red light.

- Keep enough gas for emergencies.

- Note the location of telephones so you are familiar with their location *before* you need them.

- If you are followed by another car, drive to a police or fire station, hospital emergency entrance, or any open business or gas station. Do not go home or to a friend's house. If necessary, call attention to yourself. If your car breaks down far away from help, stay in your car with your doors locked and windows closed. Ask people who stop to call the local police, your automobile club, or a friend or family member. *Do not ride with strangers.*

- If your car breaks down on campus or you lock your keys inside your car, call the University Police for motorist assistance.

- If your car fails for any reason, wait in your car for police help. Emergency police signal banners and windshield sun shades are available which can be displayed in your rear window to alert other drivers to your need for assistance. These items can be purchased in almost any grocery, auto or drug store. Few potential attackers will approach you if they know that the police have been called. Stay in your car, lock your doors, and wait for safe help.

- Police officers and tow truck drivers carry identification. Do not unlock your car door or exit your vehicle until they show you their identification through the glass of your closed window.

Hitch Hiking

- Hitch hiking is dangerous. *Never Hitch Hike.*

CAMPUS SECURITY AND TRAUMA PLANS

Each college should prepare a physical Security Plan and a Crises Plan addressed to the unique character and problems of their particular campus and student situation. An outline and suggested physical Security Plan for colleges can be seen in Appendix I. Colleges can follow the principles of the Crises Plan described for schools in Chapter One. The later chapters of this book provide more detail on the contents of Trauma Plans.

CHAPTER 4

HOSPITALS AND MEDICAL CLINICS

LOS ANGELES – COUNTY/USC HOSPITAL

The day started as usual in poorly ventilated Room 1050, one of the three emergency rooms at the Los Angeles County-USC (University of Southern California) Medical Center. It was Monday, February 8, 1993. Room 1050, known as an Ambulatory Care Unit, was for walk-ins and was crowded as usual with over 100 patients waiting patiently, some not so patiently, to be interviewed by one of three triage doctors sitting in a partitioned cubicle at desks near the door. The doctors would decide which patients were seriously ill and would get emergency treatment, and which would have to wait until later for assistance. Some would wait all day to be seen.

Patients in the huge 2,045-bed medical complex are generally poor, have no medical insurance, and go to the County-USC hospital because they are likely to be very sick. In California, six million people lack health insurance and 2.7 million live in Los Angeles County. Most of them are very sick. The hospital serves up to 15,000 patients a day and is the largest of the County's six public hospitals.

The *Los Angeles Times* reported that at about 12:20 p.m. one disgruntled patient, wearing a camouflage jacket, showed his agitation by pacing up and down the room for about 10 minutes. He suddenly stopped and shouted, "Goddamn, give me something for my pain! Can't you give me something for my pain?" Hope Flynn, a patient, said the man walked up to the doctors near the door and without speaking to them opened fire with what was described as "a rain of bullets." Seven shots were fired at the staff.

Another patient, Arturo Castaneda, reported that, "He was coming, you know, he had the look of the devil in him." Another said, "He came in very calm. He stopped in front of the desk and started shooting. I jumped to the floor and everybody started running."

All three doctors were hit and critically wounded. They were Drs. Glen Rogers, 45, Paul Kazubowski, 44, and Richard May, 47. The gunman, identified later, was Damacio Ybarra Torres, 40. Hospital security guards hearing the shooting pursued Torres from the emergency room to a first-floor X-ray room were he took two hostages — Lilly Bragg, 54, a receptionist, and Doctor Anne Tournay, 32, who was spending her first day on the job. He handcuffed the two women to his wrists and barricaded himself and the two women in the room.

Negotiations went on sporadically that afternoon until 5.08 p.m. when Torres was finally persuaded to release the hostages. They were shaken, but not harmed physically. The police took a 44-caliber Magnum revolver, a 38-caliber automatic pistol, a sawed-off rifle, and a 10" Marine Corps knife from Torres.

The shooting and violence forced the hospital to shut down the emergency room to non-emergency cases for two days. But no evacuation of patients took place in the rest of the hospital.

Dr. Glenn Rogers, an internist by training, had worked two years at County-USC. He was hit in the chest with a 38-caliber bullet. He stated later from his hospital bed that he was about to ask an elderly woman about her ailments when he heard a blast rip through the room. "All of a sudden there was a tremendous explosion and I was knocked back a few inches, and my eyes closed. And then, when I opened them again I saw a man pointing a gun at me, and I realized I had been shot." Dr. Rogers ducked quickly to his left, waiting for another shot, but it didn't come. At that moment the gunman swung around eyeing other targets. Rogers recalled thinking to himself, "Well, this is my time to leave." He thought that there was going to be more shooting and that he had to get out of there to survive. "I didn't think anything heroic. I just thought, 'I've got to save myself.'"

He jumped from his chair, and holding his hand over his bleeding chest, ran into the emergency room behind him. "Help me, I've been shot," he shouted. He lay down on the floor knowing that he needed to stabilize his blood pressure by lying still. He felt weak and faint. The bullet had entered his chest on the right side, circled around inside his body and stopped close to his heart. It shattered inside Rogers, but did not sever any major blood vessels. However, he lost half of his blood supply. Dr. Rogers was treated promptly with the other two doctors and taken to the USC University Hospital nearby where he recovered enough to go home after more than a week.

The most critically injured of the three was Dr. Richard May. He had been shot in the head and body. Dr. Paul Kazubowski was on the critical list at first, but after a few days was upgraded to serious. Immediately after the shooting, nurse Timothy Dufelmeier risked his life to drag Dr. May out of the line of fire.

Hospital officials called in psychologists to help the two taken hostage and other employees to cope with the emotional trauma from the shootings. The next day Dr. Gail Anderson, chairman of the Department of Emergency Medicine at County-USC, spoke of the reactions of the employees, "There is a mood of fear. Most people are reluctant to go back to work, especially in the emergency room, unless security is improved. What I sensed this morning was anxiety."

Was This Violence Unexpected?

The doctors and staff who worked in the emergency rooms were not surprised at the violence. In fact, they had been expecting something like this to happen and had joked about which one would be the first to be shot by an angry patient. During the first six months of 1991 at the County-USC hospital, security guards responded to 1,400 reports of threats or attacks. Six arrests were made. One assailant, a panhandler, approached four nurses in the cafeteria and stabbed one of them in the neck with a pair of suture-removal scissors. Other nurses said that they have been shoved, hit, and verbally abused by patients and family members upset by long waits.

An official of the county nurses' union, Bob McCloskey, said that inadequate security at the hospital was a major issue in strikes by nurses in 1989 and 1991. Despite a beefed-up security budget at all county hospitals, McClosky said that there are many unguarded doors and routes to the emergency area.

Nurse Vicki Miller said that she had been threatened with a gun and a knife in two separate attacks three years ago. A clerical worker, Ruby Brown, described it as a "War Zone" in there (the emergency room). She saw a patient hit a doctor with a telephone. Another emergency room nurse, Ken Wong, fought off a female patient who tried to stab him with a glass dagger.

Dr. Rogers' View of Violence

While recovering in the hospital Dr. Rogers was interviewed by a *Los Angeles Times* reporter about his views on the violence in hospitals. Rogers said that he thought that Americans were crazy to allow their citizens to walk around so heavily armed. The violence caused him to think about moving to another country. "In my kind of world this would not have happened, because I would eliminate virtually all handguns from the country if I could."

Rogers also said he was disgusted with the country's health care system. He favored a system like Canada's where physicians remain in the private sector but the health insurance system is nationalized. He believed that the American system was too haphazard.

1991 Hospital Study

A week after the County-USC Hospital shooting, it came out in the local newspapers that an official 1991 study warned about the security problems in the county's hospital system. The Los Angeles County Board of Supervisors had ordered the study which was made public in June 1991. It pointed out a number of problems and proposed several actions to prevent violence at the county's hospitals:

- Access to the hospital must be strictly controlled.
- All personnel must wear security badges.
- There must be restriction of entry to the hospital by non-employees.
- All visitors to the building must be registered and issued passes.
- An electronic surveillance system and metal detectors must be installed in the psychiatric ward.
- Greater security must be used in the hospital's parking facility.

- There is a need to hire more security personnel, known as Safety Police.

Two of the L. A. County hospitals had made changes, Martin Luther King Jr./Drew Medical Center in Watts and Olive View Medical Center in Sylmar. They installed bulletproof glass between patients and the triage nurses.

The 1991 report described how bad the overcrowded conditions were in the emergency room waiting area and in the triage and pre-admittance areas. The report stated, "These conditions are the breeding grounds of disturbances, which are generated by long waiting periods, frayed tempers and exasperation. No efforts to console or placate these waiting persons is made by hospital personnel. The inevitable result is a hostile outbreak resulting in Safety Police Officer's involvement."

The *Los Angeles Times* reported that the Health Department Director had not read the report before County Supervisor Gloria Molina made it public. Most of the suggestions in the hospital report were ignored and not implemented. Shortly after the shooting it was announced that 35 additional Safety Police Officers were to be added to the hospital. One of the reasons given by officials for not implementing some of the Report's suggestions was the shortage of funds in the budget.

Who Was Damacio Ybarra Torres?

While Torres was holding two hostages, he told police in telephone conversations that "It's their turn to wait. They made me wait. I'm going to make them wait." After Torres was arrested, he told detectives that he wanted to exact revenge against a medical establishment that he accused of negligent treatment. He did not know his victims and did not ask about their conditions. Actually, Torres had been seen twice by Dr. Rogers in the past.

After police identified Torres, they searched his room at the Ford hotel near Los Angeles' Skid Row. The room showed that the man collected weapons and military paraphernalia. They found a .44-caliber rifle in addition to the weapons taken from him at the hospital. Other artifacts included a gas mask, a German helmet, manuals titled, "Boobytrap" and "Survival," camouflage clothing, and three pairs of military boots. One sticker on a cabinet stated, "I'm the NRA."

Torres had lived in a small room at the Ford Hotel for five years or more and paid $260 a month rent. He was an enigmatic man who was unemployed, except for occasional odd jobs. He lived alone, had never served in the military, had no criminal record, and apparently showed no hostility with people who knew him. His only source of steady funds was from General Relief welfare payments. He appeared to be a loner who kept to himself.

HOSPITAL VIOLENCE

Was the violence occurring in County-USC Hospital rare and unusual? Not at all. In a 1992 survey of 103 hospitals in Los Angeles and four other California metropolitan areas by the California Emergency Nurses Association, nearly 60% of the staff members of the hospitals had suffered injuries from visitors or patients, and that guns and knives were the most commonly used weapons. The study found that prolonged waits were a major trigger of violent episodes. Drunk or drug-intoxicated patients were also violence-prone as were some patients with psychiatric illnesses.

A study by the *Journal of the American Medical Association* found that there were cases of patients at San Francisco General Hospital waiting 17 hours. Patients at the Harbor/UCLA hospital waited an average of 6.4 hours, but many waited over 10 hours. Anyone would be agitated and angry after waits of these magnitudes. It's still no excuse to bring guns and knives to use against the staff.

The American Hospital Association reported that in fiscal year 1991/92, L. A. County-USC Medical Center had 423,549 outpatient visits and 247,109 emergency room visits. Nationwide at all public hospitals, (1,429) there were 67.7 million outpatient visits and 17.9 million emergency visits.

CALIFORNIA HOSPITALS

- In 1991, at the Fairview Developmental Center Costa Mesa, a painter who was angry with the administrators for not doing something about tensions within his division, shot and killed a facilities supervisor and wounded two others.

- In 1991, a pregnant woman inside the White Memorial Hospital in Boyle Heights in Los Angeles was hit by shotgun pellets fired by gang gunfire through the windows.

- In 1990, a gunman killed one woman and shot another several times at the UCLA Medical Center.

- In 1990, while 20 youths were visiting patients at County-USC, a fight broke out between gang members and an 18-year-old was shot in the face.

- The Martin Luther King Jr./Drew Medical Center was practically under siege in 1988 when five carloads of gang members converged on the lobby of the emergency room and terrorized people in the waiting room.

- In 1984 a patient at County-USC Medical Center was shot to death by a security guard in the emergency room after he reached up from his gurney, grabbed another guard's gun and opened fire.

- San Bernardino County: A patient in the San Bernardino County Hospital was killed in bed on Christmas Eve 1992.

Other violent incidents occur daily in California hospitals. Many problems stem from homeless and mentally ill persons who are not receiving adequate health care.

VIOLENCE IN OTHER PARTS OF THE U.S.A.

In a study of hospital crime in 1989 in 300 hospitals across the country, it was found that there was a sharp upswing in assaults in hospitals and that half of them took place in emergency rooms. In a 1991 study of 1,200 emergency room nurses, two out of three reported that during their careers, they had been assaulted.

NEW YORK CITY

New York City hospitals have had problems with violence for years. In 1988, an estimated 1,000 felonies and 2,700 misdemeanors occurred in New York City hospitals. No one knows how many other crimes were actually committed, but not reported.

Bellevue Hospital

New Yorkers were shocked to read in the newspapers about the tragic murder of Dr. Kathryn Hinnant, a 33-year-old pathologist in her office in Bellevue Hospital on January 7, 1989. It wasn't until the next day that her husband and a security officer found her. She had been beaten, raped, and strangled to death.

A few days later Steven Smith was turned into the police by some homeless men. Smith apparently had been living in Bellevue for about a week and making rounds of the hospital as a doctor. He survived by stealing food from patient rooms and sleeping in empty rooms.

A SYNOPSIS

Louisville

A University of Louisville survey in 1988 of 127 emergency rooms found that 41 reported at least one verbal threat a day, 23 received at least one armed threat a month, and 55 sustained at least one physical attack a month.

Chicago

- In 1982, a woman being treated at the University of Chicago Medical Center in Hyde Park was raped in her hospital room.

- A security guard was found beaten to death in a hallway of the Loyola University Medical Center near Maywood in 1982.

- In 1985, a food service supervisor at Rush-Presbyterian-St. Luke's Medical Center was assaulted and left bound and gagged on a hospital stairwell.

Salt Lake City

- In 1991, a 39 year-old Utah man, angry because doctors had performed sterilization surgery on his wife, stormed a suburban hospital, armed with dynamite and two guns. He killed a nurse and held eight people hostage before surrendering.

Detroit

- A 57-year-old woman, Xenia Binney, had been sitting in the reception room of the Henry Ford Hospital eye clinic about 30 minutes on July 28, 1993, when she took the elevator down 10 floors, went to her car for a few minutes, returned to the clinic, and opened fire at the staff with a .22-caliber revolver. She shot one eye clinic technician in his lower back, and then shot George Ponka another technician, three times in his chest and shoulders. Ponka lunged at Binney and knocked her down preventing her from shooting again.

She told police later that "I shot those two doctors 'cause they killed my mom." She said, "Doctors butchered my mother." Apparently Binney believed that her mother, Sophie Steinofsky, had received inadequate care at another hospital in Detroit. At the time of her mother's death, no complaints had been filed with the hospital. She did not know the two technicians that she shot.

HOSPITAL NURSERY VIOLENCE

The security of the nursery at the Corona Regional Medical Center in California was violated August 9, 1993, when a distraught woman, Sopehia White, entered the facility and allegedly pulled out a .38-caliber revolver. She ordered one nurse with a baby in her arms out of the room. She then pointed the gun at the other nurse, Elizabeth Staten, 30, and said, "You've ruined my life. You've taken my children. I have no reason to live. I'm going to kill you. Open your mouth. I'm going to stick this gun in there and blow your head off."

White allegedly shot six times hitting Staten two times in the lower left chest, the abdomen and the left index finger with two shots. Staten went downstairs, trailing blood to the emergency room entrance, where White fired two more shots, hitting Staten once.

Joan Black, an emergency room nurse, hearing the shots, went to the perpetrator, put one arm around her and with the arm put her hand over the top of the pistol to stop any more shooting and calmed her down. Black talked to her for about ten minutes until she gave up the pistol and collapsed sobbing. Black said, "She (White) was like a wounded animal. She was in agony." Black reported that she was afraid of being shot, but felt she had to help.

Baby Abductions From Hospitals

In St. Mary's Hospital, Brooklyn, NY, on October 3, 1991, a woman wearing a laboratory coat and stethoscope kidnapped a two-day-old baby girl from a bassinet in the maternity hallway. The child was on its way to the mother's room. The baby was recovered the next day when the woman took the baby to nearby St. Joseph's Hospital for a check-up.

In the Parkland Memorial Hospital, Dallas, TX, on January 24, 1993, a woman wearing hospital scrubs, mask, and a ID badge, entered a new mother's room. She told the mother that she had to take the baby for about 20 minutes to do some blood work. The mother became anxious, called nurses when the baby was not returned in one and a half hours. At that time the staff became aware of the kidnapping. After the media aired the abduction including a detailed description of the kidnapper provided by the mother, the mother-in-law of the abductor called the police and the baby was recovered.

National Abductions

Abductions by non-family members from hospitals of newborns/infants (birth through six months) is a serious problem that concerns hospital authorities throughout the country. The National Center for Missing & Exploited Children keeps tabs of newborn/infant abductions that occur nationally. In an August 3, 1993, memorandum they indicated that the number of abductions of infants from 1983-1993 totaled 126 of which 80 were taken from hospitals. To date 76 infants kidnapped from hospitals were located and 4 are missing. Of the 80 abductions, 57 percent were taken from a mother's room; 16 percent from a nursery; 16 percent from pediatrics; and 11 percent from "on premises." But there is some good news. Because of national proactive education programs, infant abductions from hospitals actually decreased 55 percent in 1992.

In a publication entitled, *For Hospital Professionals: Guidelines on Preventing Infant Abductions,* by John B. Rabun, Jr., of the National Center For Missing & Exploited Children, a profile of the typical perpetrator was given:

"The offender is almost always a female, frequently overweight, ranges in age from 14 to 45 years, and generally has no prior criminal record. . . . While she appears 'normal,' the woman is most likely compulsive, suffers from low self-esteem, often fakes one or more pregnancies, and relies on manipulation and lying as a coping mechanism in her interpersonal relationships. Often she wishes either to 'replace' an infant she has lost or to experience a 'vicarious birthing' of a child she is for some reason unable to conceive or carry to term. The baby may be used in an attempt to maintain/save a relationship with her husband, boyfriend, or companion. . . The race/skin color of the abductor almost always matches the infant's or reflects that of the abductor's significant other."

RURAL HOSPITALS

Even small rural hospitals can't escape violence.

North Carolina

In 1987, in a small rural hospital in North Carolina, Dr. Perry McLimore worked the emergency room alone. A patient, who six years earlier had been denied a prescription for sleeping pills by the doctor, stole silently into the room where Dr. McLimore worked. His motive – revenge. Even though the man had been drunk when he was denied the sleeping pills, he felt slighted. He had carried his anger inside for six years before returning to stalk Dr. McLimore and get even.

Out of the corner of his eye, Perry McLimore spotted the man and his gun. He tried to duck, grabbing a curtain for cover. The bullet grazed his left shoulder as two State

Troopers entered the emergency room on police business. Dr. McLimore watched as they engaged in gun fire and killed the perpetrator. Because there were no other doctors available, McLimore returned and finished his shift. Even though the veteran emergency physician had just been shot by a drunk gunman and watched him killed before his eyes, he did not take the rest of the night off. "I couldn't find anybody on such short notice and I really wasn't hurt that bad. The wound itself was nothing and I was supposed to stay until seven that morning." he said.

Emergency room physicians are sometimes known as a rough-and-ready crew. They stake their honor on being able to handle any crisis. Most thrive on the excitement of emergency decision making in times of life and death crises.

Joshua Tree, California

On May 16, 1993, the San Bernardino County Sheriff's Department was called to the Hi-Desert Medical Center to investigate a disturbance by a man in the emergency room. While a sheriff's sergeant was attempting to escort David Chism, 28, out of the hospital, he grabbed the sergeant's baton and hit him with it on the head, shoulders, and arms.

The sergeant then pulled out his gun and ordered Chism to drop the baton. When Chism moved toward the sergeant in a threatening manner, the deputy opened fire and killed him. Authorities gave no reason as to why Chism was causing a distrubance.

ABORTION CLINICS

Pensacola, Florida

During a Sunday service, Michael Frederick Griffin, 31, of Pensacola, offered a prayer for Dr. David Gunn, 47, at the Whitfield Assembly of God Church. Griffin then offered up his own life to Jesus before joining an abortion protest group outside the Women's Medical Services Clinic on March 11, 1993. Several members of Rescue America said they heard Griffin yell to the doctor "Don't kill any more babies!" At about 10:00 AM, as Dr. Gunn left his car and approached the entrance to the clinic, Griffin suddenly pulled out a hand gun and shot the doctor in the chest several times.

Dr. Gunn, the first doctor slain during an anti-abortion protest since the procedure was legalized 20 years ago, was buried in his home town of Winchester, Tennessee. Dr. Gunn's son explained that recently his father had changed his routes to work because the threats against him were increasing. "When I asked him if it was worth it, he told me not to worry and that it wouldn't come to that," his son said. "I guess he had too much faith in people."

Over a dozen anti-abortion protesters gathered in front of the clinic witnessed the shooting. Griffin was arrested and charged with murder. Friends of Griffin described him as a man of hidden passions but extremist views. According to court documents, Griffin had a long standing propensity for violence, a loner's mentality and an ability to stubbornly resist reason and logic once he decided on a position.

In a 1991 divorce petition, Griffin's former wife alleged that her husband of ten years suffered from "great fits of violence." She also said he'd threatened to take away their two daughters, stating that if he couldn't have them, neither of them would. She obtained a restraining order against him, but they finally reconciled.

Melbourne, Florida

In March of 1993 , protesters stood 50 feet from the door of the small Aware Woman's Clinic just south of Cape Canaveral, Florida for weeks and condemned as "baby killers" the three experienced doctors on the clinic's staff. Large posters portraying "Wanted - Child Killers" were distributed thoughout the doctors' home neighborhoods. These posters included personal information such as home phone numbers and details about their children, spouses, and parents. The protestors blocked driveways, followed the doctors on their way to work and sometimes tried to run them off the road at night. Fearing deadly attacks, two of the doctors on the staff finally quit.

HOSPITAL DOWNSIZING

The nation's hospital staffs in 1993 faced new stress from downsizing of their facilities. Because of severe budget problems in California due to the economy and changing medical care delivery systems, it was announced in June 1993, that state hospitals would face serious lay-offs. The Director of the big Camarillo State Hospital and Developmental Center said that at least 90 employees of the 1,800 staff would be cut. The list included nurses, psychiatric technicians, physicians, psychologists, rehabilitation therapists, plumbers, painters, clerical workers, and a cook.

David Freehauf, the hospital director, said more cuts might come if county mental health departments choose to send acutely ill patients to cheaper private and public programs rather than to the state hospital. State costs approach $100,000 per patient per year. Budget problems throughout the state were causing hospitals and mental health departments to find cheaper ways to care for patients and find funds. Staff members facing job loss were worried and feeling the stress of not knowing where they would find a job. State hospital staffs in other parts of the country were facing similar problems.

EMERGENCY ROOM STUDIES

In a study made of the amount of violence in Emergency Departments or Emergency Rooms (referred to as ERs in text) of teaching hospitals in the U.S., it was found that 43 percent of the hospitals reported that their medical staff were physically attacked on an average of once a month, and that seven percent of these attacks resulted in a death.

In the first six months after a metal detector arch was installed at the Henry Ford Hospital in Detroit, authorities detected 33 handguns, 1,234 knives, and many other hazardous items. In a Los Angeles inner-city hospital the officials found that approximately 25 percent of the male trauma patients and 31 percent of the female patients have weapons with them when admitted to the ER.

Scary isn't it? Not only do ER personnel need to know how to treat injured patients, but they need to be trained to handle violent acts from their patients and/or relatives and visitors. Unfortunately, not all ER staff are trained to identify and cope with hostile people. Violence against health care workers falls into two general categories: violence by abusive and assaultive patients, and violence by visitors.

IDENTIFYING AND MANAGING VIOLENT PERPETRATORS

Hospitals need to prepare plans for identifying potential violent persons, defusing them, and/or calling for help. Unfortunately, they need to consider all patients and visitors as potentially dangerous. In particular they need to keep an eye on people in waiting rooms who show agitation, pace, advance and retreat from the staff, clench their fists, make facial grimaces, speak loudly, or challenge the staff's authority.

Reliance on Technology vs Basic Human Kindness

It is important that hospitals take steps to protect staffs and patients, but it's a myth that locked doors, bulletproof glass, and alarm buttons, etc., will ensure no violence. People can still be violent once they are behind barriers. Staff need to be alert and keep potential weapons — scalpels, needles, and other instruments that can be used as weapons away from patients.

Prompt response and basic kindness with patients can go far in preventing patient hostility and violent behavior.

SUGGESTIONS FOR COPING WITH AGITATED PATIENTS

1. Don't ignore aggressive behavior. Some of the worst hospital shootings have come from impatient patients. Staff should take intervention steps quickly.

2. Let the patient express his/her irritation (verbally).

3. Listen to the patient. Speak in calm, short sentences.

4. Don't look the patient in the eye. This can be taken as a confrontational act.

5. Don't argue with the patient about his complaints.

6. Check for weapons. Loose clothing can hide weapons. Check people who walk stiff legged — they may have a rifle stuffed in their pant leg. In general, only specifically trained people should approach hostile patients or visitors to check for weapons. There must be a policy for removing and storing weapons when found.

7. Major trauma victims should be undressed as soon as possible and any weapons, matches or cigarette lighters removed.

8. Give regular updates to patients when long waits are unavoidable. Don't say, "It'll be 15 minutes." This approach reduces clock watching.

9. Only one person should deal with an agitated patient. Have continuity of communication.

10. Activate a call for help when aggressive behavior begins. The call can always be cancelled if the situation is defused.

SECURITY PLAN FOR ERs

Hospitals should have a physical security plan if sufficient danger exists or potential danger is possible. As security costs a lot of money, each hospital should weigh the costs of their needs against the physical environment that will be created after facilities and services are in place. In other words, analyze the impact on the ER operation of costly security measures after large sums are spent to install them.

- All unnecessary doors to the hospital and ER should be locked and access to the hospital limited to just a few controlled or patrolled entrances.

- Surveillance closed-circuit television monitors should cover the entrances, waiting room, especially parking lots, and immediate hospital grounds.

- Hospital staff should have two or more methods of communicating with the police or security personnel. ER staff should have access to at least two telephone lines, in different locations, in case the hospital telephone service is disrupted by an intruder. One line should be an outside line and not go through the hospital operator. An extra line is not necessary if cellular phones are used.

- Access doors to the ER should be capable of being locked to keep out a perpetrator or even gangs who have entered an ER to attack a previous victim or for some other reason. The paramedic medical communications room should be capable of being locked from the inside.

Other preventive strategies include warning police officers to come well armed. Many of the gangs come into emergency rooms armed with submachine guns and automatic rifles in addition to handguns. Some hospital authorities believe that the 38-caliber pistols that many security guards use are dangerous because they are so inaccurate and do not provide adequate protection when a staff is under threat. Some experienced hospital officers recommend that a 12-gauge shotgun is imposing and effective if used by a highly trained person.

Restraints

Each hospital should have a policy in place concerning what type of chemical or physical restraints to use on a violent person. Don't approach a hostile person unless you have sufficient personnel. Take a team approach and three to five strong individuals, to restrain a person with hard leather or other physical restraints. Avoid using a strait-jacket as it is undesirable — it gets hot, causes claustrophobia, the person becomes anxious, and it denies access to body parts for examination and treatment.

CALIFORNIA EMERGENCY NURSES ASSOCIATION TAKE ACTION

On April 15, 1990, Debbie Burke, RN, was killed in the emergency room of the Mission Bay Memorial Hospital in San Diego by a man distraught over the death of his father who died in surgery in the hospital the previous day. The man entered the emergency room and fired a barrage of bullets from a hand gun that killed Burke, an emergency medical technician student, the Emergency Room physician on duty, and another patients's father.

Not only was the community angry over the senseless killing, but so were emergency room nurses throughout California. Shortly after the tragedy, the California Emergency Nurses Association's Government Affairs Committee decided to conduct a survey to determine the following:

1. The magnitude of violence against emergency room nurses,

2. Current practices in effect to deal with aggressive or violent behavior, and

3. Current security practices within institutions.

Interviews were conducted with nurse managers in five metropolitan areas — Sacramento, San Francisco, Fresno, Los Angeles, and San Diego. The study included hospitals in the inner-city, 10 percent, urban, 60 percent, and rural, 30 percent. Thirty percent of the hospitals were public and 70 percent were private. In general, survey takers believed that nurse managers downplayed the magnitude of violence just as hospital administrators tend to downplay trouble in their facility.

One of the major findings was that the majority of emergency rooms did **not** have gang and drug activity in the area served by the hospital, yet experienced considerable violence in their ERs. It appeared to be a myth that violence occurs primarily in areas infested with gangs and drugs. A second finding was that although most incidents were threats — verbal and physical (without a weapon) — actual acts of violence were also occurring. Most of the violence was directed at staff members, resulting in mostly minor injuries but necessitating several days off from work. In several instances severe injuries occurred.

Practices and measures to protect staff varied considerably. Some hospitals had policies for dealing with violent persons, but employees lacked training in recognizing and dealing with dangerous individuals. The study disclosed that violence is primarily associated with substance abuse, psychiatric illness, patient anger, and prolonged waiting times.

A majority of hospitals had some sort of preventive measure to protect ER staff. The most common means were a locked unit and security officers. The nurse managers were not impressed with the quality of the hospital security officers. They believed that the officers were not sufficiently trained and would not be able to respond adequately in an emergency situation.

Over half of all ERs surveyed reported incidents that involved weapons brought into the ER by patients or visitors — usually knives and loaded guns. In most facilities, after an aggressive patient was recognized, few were searched.

RECOMMENDATIONS

After reviewing the survey, the Government Affairs Committee in April, 1991, recommended a policy for an action plan for hospitals and ERs. Their four points were:

- Establish guidelines for minimal safety features, but use existing hospital Safty Committees to assess the need for security improvements and changes.

- Establish minimal educational requirements for personnel working within the emergency room.

- Establish minimal training standards for security personnel working in health care facilities and the provision of sufficient equipment.

- Establish reporting requirements and criminal penalties for persons carrying out violent acts against health care workers who are performing their duties.

Following the adoption of the policy, the California Emergency Nurses' Association prepared a bill that national members could introduce to their state legislatures to give teeth to their recommended plan. Please see the Bill in Appendix III. Contact the Bill Room at the California State capitol for a copy.

COPING WITH VIOLENT PATIENTS AND VISITORS

Why Do Emergency Rooms have Violence?

To provide quick and easy access to emergency care, most ERs provide several means of access — for emergency vehicles, waiting room patients, and staff. This makes the area easily accessible to outsiders. Many of the patients brought into ERs for treatment have been beaten, knifed, shot, or have taken part in violence themselves. As pointed out before, many of the patients are poor, have endured long waits and are under a lot of stress. Unfortunately, ER staff must consider all patients and visitors as potentially violent and maintain a vigil over them.

Identifying a Potentially Violent Patient/Visitor.

Many hospital ERs such as San Gorgonio Memorial Hospital in Banning, California, have established profiles of potential perpetrators and policies to follow, shown below, if a patient or visitor becomes violent. Harriet Gray, RN, Safety Director, developed a "Code Gray" that summons immediate help if the patient:

- Talks and complains loudly, uses profanity, and makes sexual comments.
- Makes unnecessary demands for services.
- Says that he/she is going to lose control.
- Paces about the waiting room.
- Appears very tense and angry.
- Challenges authority.
- Appears to be drunk or under the influence or drugs.
- Has a history of previous violence.

Action to Take with a Threatening or Potentially Violent Person:

Each hospital should prepare written policy and training for staff for coping with potentially violent persons and review the policy at regular intervals. The following is suggested:

- Don't argue or provoke the hostile person. Some eye contact may be OK, but avoid staring at the person. It could be taken as a confrontational act.
- Be honest about the situation and explain reason for any delays.
- Any comments should be about the patient's behavior and not about him/her personally.

- Keep at least two to three arms length away from the hostile person and don't allow yourself to be backed into a corner. Leave room for your escape if necessary.
- Talk to person in a firm tone of voice, make sentences short and direct.
- Listen and acknowledge your concern for the person's anger. Don't accept the blame for any of the accusations made.
- Don't touch the patient unless necessary and only after telling him/her what you are going to do.
- Keep the patient separated from other patients and in another room if possible.
- Check for weapons.
- Attempt no heroic attempts to subdue or control patient.
- Don't lie to them!
- Don't be disrespectful to gang leaders, if in the waiting room — acknowledge their postion of authority.
- Call a suitable warning Code or similar emergency code to alert security and hospital staff to a threat. The Code will trigger a rapid response from trained personnel in the hospital to report to the area with the problem. Each code should have a response plan.

Action to Take When Violence Does Erupt.

- Call an emergency code signifying a violent person.
- Call security and/or police, 911.
- Do not attempt to subdue the person yourself.
- Give the patient drugs if he/she demands them.
- Keep other patients away from incident and areas.
- Report episodes of verbal and physical abuse.

- Debrief all episodes of violence to learn, "What could be done better" the next time.

ACTION HOSPITALS CAN TAKE TO PREVENT VIOLENCE

Each hospital should survey their facilities for security strengths and weaknesses and prepare a security plan based on points similar to those outlined below. As some security measures are expensive, administrators may have to set priorities for equipment and services and install them as money becomes available. However, many safety features are simple and not costly. A summary of major actions for hospitals, especially ERs and including the department of obstetrics, to take to prevent violence are:

- Identify problems and danger points within and near hospital.
- Issue badges to all visitors and patients.
- Issue identification tags to all staff members, doctors, nurses, assistants, etc.
- Develop procedures for processing all patients faster at emergency room waiting room, especially ones meeting the profile of a dangerous person.
- Make waiting rooms pleasant if budget constraints prevent moving patients faster through triage admittance.
- Isolate emergency room from waiting room with security doors or locked door/partition. Use barriers (bulletproof vests, locked doors) judiciously. The more barriers for patients, the more frustration people develop.
- Install bulletproof windows between triage nurses and patients in waiting room or relocate triage area.
- Install metal detecting devices.
- Install surveillance cameras.

- Establish communication system within ER area with separate line or a cellular phone in case hospital telephone system fails. Check communication system. Find ways to alert other hospital departments that someone is agitated in the hospital. Don't keep it a secret.

- Improve lighting in parking lots and areas surrounding hospital.

- Hire security or Safety Policemen trained to handle problems within emergency room area.

- Establish arrangements with police to respond quickly to calls about a violent patient, visitor, or gang in ER. Use A.K.A. (Also Known As) names for all police officers, gang members, and criminals admitted for treatment.

- Provide appropriate training for employees and security measures such as "screamers," panic buttons, and electronic personal alarm devices.

- Other security measures include electronic tracking systems for staff such as magnetic keyed name tags, staff lock outs from areas like the pharmacy, etc. Other measures include security guards on bicycles and with dogs.

A more detailed security outline entitled, "Emergency Department Public Safety Survey Procedures" can be seen in Appendix IV. In summary, it is important that security plans be prepared in relationship with other departments. But every department need not have the same security system as the ER. What's good for the cafeteria may not be appropriate for the obstetrics department. Security plans should be tailored for the unique needs of each department. There is a need for balance. Analyze the benefits from investing in additional staff, training, and prompt care versus more security hardware. Good design can improve security and produce a pleasant environment.

CHAPTER 5

GOVERNMENT OFFICES, COURTS, POST OFFICES & PUBLIC PLACES

STATE GOVERNMENT FACILITIES

STATE TAX AGENCY

The drama began early in the morning when Ray Holloway, 53, tried to get past security at the California State Board of Equalization building in Sacramento by flashing his badge. When he was refused entrance, he returned to his van in the parking lot where another security guard confronted him. Holloway pulled a gun, disarmed and handcuffed the guard, and returned to the building. He aimed his shotgun at the guard stationed behind a glass partition until the guard released the locks to the building. An alarm was set off and Holloway fired several times into the guard booth. He then made his way to the 18th floor while pursued by a state police officer. Once on the floor he took 18 hostages and told them he had no intention of being captured alive. He demanded to know the whereabouts of seven state employees on a list he had brought with him.

After a standoff of several hours, a barrage of state police exchanged fire with Holloway. He was killed in the skirmish.

It was discovered later that when Holloway had transferred to the Department of Alcohol Beverage Control (ABC) in 1972 as a special investigator, he had problems within the group. In the 1980s he was disciplined for frightening a group of campers with a firearm and for getting drunk. His salary was cut by five percent for a year after authorities discovered he had filed false daily reports saying he was working when he was absent from the job. Frustrated over his personal tax problems, Holloway told hostages at the Board of Equalization that he was having trouble with back taxes. He demanded to see a particular employee of the Board of Equalization but the employee, whose office was responsible for sending letters regarding delinquent or incomplete tax returns, had retired previously.

Twenty-three-hundred state workers were evacuated from the high-rise building, seven blocks from the State Capitol during the incident. Ray Holloway went to the Board with a shotgun, a carbine rife, a .45-caliber pistol and a revolver to resolve the problem. Holloway had previously been a California Highway Patrol Officer from 1966 to 1972. He then transferred to the State Dept. of Alcoholic Beverage Control as an investigator. Holloway held a license to sell beer and wine in Milpitas, California. It was believed the tax problems he was having related to this license.

PUBLIC SOCIAL SERVICES

Los Angeles

In February 1993, a social worker at the Los Angeles County Public Social Services agency, who had been fired from her job in Santa Fe Springs over a year ago, walked into her former office and shot the supervisor, Thu

Nguyen, who had previously made the decision to terminate her. The assailant, Wanda Rogers, 43, surrendered later at a San Bernardino County Sheriff's Station about 50 miles east of Los Angeles.

Witnesses said that Rogers walked past a group of people celebrating a baby shower on her way to Nguyen's cubicle. She fired a single shot at close range and other employees thought it was a balloon popping. She then got in her car and drove away. It was thought that the termination was the motive for the shooting.

The victim, Thu Nguyen, 53, was flown to a nearby hospital and treated for gunshot wounds. Fortunately, he survived.

Michigan

In April 1993, Barbara Synnestvedt, 46, a social worker at the W.J. Maxey Training School for juveniles near Whitmore Lake, Michigan, was beaten and strangled to death. She was found in an employees' lounge. A 19-year-old-man, Jermell Darnell Johnson, was charged with the murder. He had been sent to the Maxey school after a conviction for rape. The Michigan State Department of Social Services was looking into the slaying and reviewing the security system at the school.

In another city in Michigan, Rebecca Binkowski, 25, a Master of Social Worker student was found stabbed to death in her car in February 1993. She was the resident manager at the Kalamazoo Township apartment house for mentally ill people. A resident of the Township house, David Stappenbeck, 24, was charged with the murder.

Binkowski was awarded her MSW degree posthumously and a scholarship established in her name. Since both suspects were clients of the two women, the state social worker chapter was concerned about adequate safety of their members at public workplaces.

Watkins Glen, NY

John T. Miller of Ohio was behind in child support payments. He owed $6,780 to Schuyler County for support of a now-grown child that he denied he ever fathered. For the first time, $51 was withheld from his paycheck. This apparently triggered a violent reaction. On October 15, 1992, he walked into the child support unit and shot and killed four social workers, four-fifths of the staff.

Mary Ellen Upham, the fifth social worker, happened to be out of the office at the time of the shooting. Miller had been in the office the day before the shooting, but apparently made no threats or gave any outward indication that intended to kill any of them. The child support staff had asked for greater security for their unit, but never got it. Beverly Clickner, who has an office next to the child support unit said, "We're threatened all the time, and sometimes we're not taken very seriously." Upham reported that there is no way to lock their office doors from inside, no escape routes, and visitors can gain entrance by way of a back door as Miller did.

EMPLOYMENT DEVELOPMENT AGENCY

Nevada

Apparently angered because he had recently lost his disability benefits, a man walked into the state insurance office in Las Vegas, July 8, 1993, and opened fire with two blasts to the ceiling with a shotgun. Witnesses reported that the man shouted, "I'm sick of this and I'm not going to take it any more!" and started shooting. He then got into his truck and drove inside the building and started shooting again. Three people received minor injuries, but not from any of the gunshots.

Workers and visitors were screaming, running to get away—some even jumped through windows. A security guard shot the perpetrator in the head while he was shooting from his truck. He was taken to the University Medical Center where he underwent surgery. Later, the man was identified as Jim Forrester, 58.

California

The California State Employment Development Department had a bad year in 1986. On March 31, in a San Bernardino County office, a claimant angry over his situation shot a supervisor in the office and then killed himself. In San Francisco on June 6, 1986, another claimant walked into the office, pulled out an army carbine, aimed at the staff and pulled the trigger several times. But the weapon didn't fire. As staff members tried to disarm him, he pulled out an axe and attacked one of the supervisors. He was able to strike the person in the head several times before he was captured. The supervisor recovered later in the hospital.

The two bad experiences were enough for the agency. They initiated a study by a task force of their physical security arrangements and policies for handling a hostile perpetrator and published a report in 1986 entitled, "Safety in the Workplace." The recommendations did bring about a revision of procedures and physical design of office spaces, primarily within job service field offices, that worked for them. Some of the major changes made are indicated below.

The Task Force's Key Findings in Working with Public

1. Office safety depends primarily on the procedures used in dealing with the public, the office's relationship with the community and the skills and attitudes of the employees. Specific physical security features are important but secondary.

2. Changes in work procedures, including automation of various functions, will provide more efficient and effec-

tive service to the public and will permit reduction in the number of in-person contacts.

Summary of Recommendations:

Office Procedures

- All clients should be escorted to and from work areas which are behind public access counters.

- The state and local police should be telephoned for immediate assistance if a situation which appears to present a physical danger arises.

- A standard notation system regarding hostile and abusive clients should be included in both paper files and computer records for claimants and job service applicants. This recording should include incidents in which clients actually committed or attempted to commit a violent act or engaged in a major disturbance.

- At the office manager's discretion, interviews with difficult clients may be assigned to supervisors, and state police or local law enforcement agencies may be notified in advance.

- Determination notices should be mailed and will carry the signature of the Director (not a staff member).

- Clients should be served as expeditiously as possible.

- A reception and forms area should be available to assist and respond to client questions, monitor waiting time, and expedite completion of forms.

- The Department should have a clearly stated policy regarding the manner in which service is provided to inebriated, hostile or abusive clients or service can be denied to problem clients.

Training

- Training in self-awareness should be provided to help employees identify behavior which clients might view as antagonistic.

- Supervisors should monitor and reinforce, on an ongoing basis, employees' interviewing skills and behavior and provide refresher training as appropriate.

Office Appearance

- Simple, attractive signs should be installed to direct clients to appropriate areas of the office.

- Sufficient chairs should be provided in lobby areas to reduce stand up waiting.

- Carpet should be installed to reduce noise in work areas, particularly in sections designated for interviews.

Office Reconfiguration

- Where possible, only a single public entryway should be available for each field office lobby.

- All desk and counter items which might be thrown by clients should be removed.

- Counters should be installed that are sufficiently wide to preclude arm reach contact and high enough to impede an attempt to jump over it.

- All counter openings should be equipped with bank-type counter-high gates with mechanical latching capability.

- A buzzer signal control should be installed at every desk where sensitive interviews are conducted. This system should be linked to a central receiver unit which identifies the point of signal origin.

- Assure that all rear or side doors preclude entry to unauthorized persons.

Incident Reporting, Risk Analysis and Department Response

- Persons who have displayed abusive, hostile or potentially violent behavior should be advised by Investigation Division staff or law enforcement officers of the serious consequences to them if they repeat such actions or threats.

CIA - WASHINGTON DC

In January of 1993, a dark, curly-haired gunman left his car in the left turn lane outside the entrance to CIA headquarters, walked between two rows of cars, stopped at a red light, and opened fire on several vehicles at point blank range. He used a weapon resembling an AK-47 assault rifle. He then returned to his car and sped away. Frank Darling, 28, and Lansing Bennett, 66, both of Reston, Virginia were killed in the incident. Police had no doubt he specifically targeted CIA employees. A roadblock was set up outside the headquarters where over 30 witnesses to the shooting were questioned. The CIA provided some names of disgruntled employees which were investigated.

During the following manhunt, a suspect, identified as Mir Aimal Kansi, a worker for a local courier service, was sought. The AK-47 used in the attack was found in his apartment. While still at large, authorities learned from the courier service where Kansi worked up until the day before the shooting, that the service is owned by the son of a former high-level CIA official. However, a definite link between the shooting and the CIA Agency was not established. To date, the suspect has not been found.

COURTHOUSE VIOLENCE

Jamestown, California

Ellie Nesler of Jamestown, California, a single mother raising two kids alone, scraped by on Welfare and money from odd jobs. On April 4, 1993, she said she had been pushed "over the edge" by events involving the trial of Daniel Mark Driver who was accused of molesting her seven-year old son at a Church camp in 1988. She just couldn't take it anymore.

Nesler and her son were scheduled to testify in court against Driver, who faced seven counts of child molestation involving Ellie's son and three other young boys, ages six to eight at the time of the molestation. The parents of the children involved had waited four years for Driver to be apprehended by law enforcement officials. Nesler described Driver as "walking into the courtroom with a big smile on his face."

That morning, Nesler's son awakened sick to his stomach in anticipation of facing the man who he said had haunted his nights for the past four years. The boy told his mother that Danny Driver threatened to kill his family if he told anyone about the "nasty things he did to me." Outside the courtroom, waiting for the trial, the boy could not stop vomiting. When Driver was led in, he caught sight of the Nesler boy throwing up into a large garbage bag and flashed a big smirk. "I looked up and he was staring at me with this funny grin on his face," the boy said.

Ellie Nesler became so enraged at the idea of Driver mocking them that she lunged at him, but family members stopped her, holding her back. Her face was flushed and her eyes were burning. She paced the hallway, trying to comfort her son, when one of the other mothers involved walked out of the courtroom shaking her head. The mother said it wasn't going well and she thought Driver was 'going to walk.' The kids were giving weak testimony. "He got to the kids again," she said.

After a short break in the trial, a sheriff's deputy led Ellie into the courtroom. Danny Driver was sitting at the near side of the table, his back to her. Without a word, she pulled out a semiautomatic handgun, pointed it at Driver, and emptied the gun chamber, missing him only once.

"There was no indication of a problem, no words exchanged," said Michael Costs, Tuolumne County Assistant Sheriff. "The deputy who escorted Nesler into the room stopped to talk to another deputy and that's when we heard the pop, pop, pop." Ellie Nesler was immediately apprehended and arrested for the shooting.

Nesler's mother described to reporters the nightmare her daughter had been through. The child's aunt did the same and told how the boy had confided the molestation by Driver to her when he attended a religious camp in the mountains where Driver worked as a dishwasher. The aunt thought the boy was acting strange. He finally asked her if she could keep a secret. "Please keep it secret, Auntie. Danny told me he would kill my sister and me and my mom if I told anyone."

After her sister told her of the boy's story, Ellie Nesler took the allegations to the authorities, but Driver had already left the area. She searched for him over the next three years while watching her son grow increasingly morose. "One minute he's sunny and open, and the next minute, he's angry and closed and in your face," she said. "He has a short fuse and he can't handle the stress of school."

Nesler sought counseling for the boy when he came home from school crying several times, saying he had seen Driver parked in his yellow Buick outside the school playground.

Driver was arrested in Palo Alto in 1989 for theft and returned to Tuolumne County to face the molestation charges. He had previously been accused of lewd acts with young boys. Five years earlier, he pleaded guilty to multiple counts of sex with boys in the San Jose area. For that charge he was given probation based on letters sent to the judge from his church, attesting to his fine character.

After the shooting Ellie Nesler became a local hero, a beacon for people everywhere angered by crime and frustrated by the legal system. Two area banks set up defense funds. Calls of support poured in from across the country, Canada, Italy, Spain, and Denmark. The trial for shooting Driver finally started in August of 1993.On August 11, 1993, Nesler was found guilty of voluntary manslaughter. In interviews after the findings, Nesler indicated that she was happy with the jury's decision.

This case shows all too tragically the need for security in courtrooms across the country. Particularly, when volatile cases, such as child molestation, divorce or other emotionally-charged cases are tried.

NATIONWIDE COURTHOUSE VIOLENCE

Courthouses around the country have been the scene of deadly violence. The recent following cases are only a sample of the actual number.

Divorce Proceedings - Family Law

The *National Law Journal* reported that in nine months of 1992 seven men distraught over their divorce proceedings shot people in courthouses killing two lawyers, three ex-wives, and two relatives, and injuring three judges, three lawyers, three sheriff's deputies, and two court personnel.

The *Law Journal* found that divorce lawyers and judges were worried about the carnage and were taking a lower profile. Some lawyers believe that divorce law has always been dangerous and that dissolving a marriage brings out the worst in people. Others think that society's recent explosion of guns and violence has reached the courtroom and that changes in divorce law in the past decade, such as no fault, has made litigants more angry and ready to strike out at the lawyers and professionals who operate the legal system.

Some lawyers thought that the actions of family law practitioners had brought on some of violence and that they were part of the problem rather than part of the solution. Judge Herbert S. Glickman, a family law judge in Newark said, "I think lawyers are slinging more mud than they should these days ... making serious and unnecessary charges."

Fort Worth, TX

In July of 1992, George Lott, 47, approached the bench in a Fort Worth courtroom, pulled out a Glock model 19 semiautomatic and started shooting. He shot and wounded two Appeals Judges and an Assistant District Attorney. He then turned and killed another Assistant District Attorney. Lott then escaped down a back stairwell where he encountered a lawyer and killed him.

Before he surrendered to police, Lott went on a television station and said he did the shooting because he was bitter over a 1990 child custody dispute. Lott, a graduate of the University of Texas Law School, said that he shot at lawyers and judges randomly because he was angry at the legal system.

Milwaukee, WI

One lawyer put the situation this way, "Criminal lawyers represent the worst people at their best. We represent the best people at their worst." Another lawyer said, "We deal with people excited, anxious, depressed, afraid."

When Circuit Judge Marianne Becker of Waukesha, near Milwaukee, was a Family Court Judge she was very guarded and protective. She told reporters at the *National Law Journal*: "I open envelopes behind me . . . the part I can most afford to lose is what I sit on." She told her children never to start her car, open doors to strangers or accept packages with excess postage. Bombers apparently make sure that their packages have enough postage. Judge Becker found, "The danger in family court is greater than criminal court."

San Bernardino, CA

While waiting for a hearing on September 24, 1992, at the San Bernardino County courthouse to end their troubled relationship, Kimberly Robinson, 25, and her live-in boyfriend, Lynn Waller, 30, got into an argument. Her father, Melvin Robinson, 45, intervened to calm down the fight. Unfortunately, Lynn Waller pulled out a handgun and shot and killed Mr. Robinson. At the sound of gunfire at 9:40 in the morning, men, women, and children in the courthouse ducked for cover.

Beaumont, TX

Kathy Lee Smith, 33, had complained to the sheriff's department internal affairs investigators that her ex-husband had been harassing her. They had divorced in 1989. She was just entering the courthouse July 20, 1992, for a meeting at the Sheriff's Department when she encountered her ex-husband, Deputy Dan Smith. An argument erupted. Deputy Smith pulled out his 9mm automatic pistol and shot his ex-wife several times and killed her.

Clayton, MO

Kenneth Baumruh, 53, was sitting calmly, apparently, near his estranged wife, Mary Louise, 46, and their lawyers, waiting for their divorce hearing to begin in court on May 5, 1992. Suddenly, Mr. Baumruh pulled a handgun out of his briefcase and shot and killed Ms. Baumruh. He then aimed and shot his own lawyer, Gary Seltzer, 39, and his ex-wife's lawyer, Walter Scott Pollard. Pollard was lucky, getting only a flesh wound. Seltzer was more seriously wounded. Mr. Baumruh then allegedly fired at others in the courtroom, including the judge. He wounded a bailiff and a security guard before being shot down and wounded by officers.

Cleveland, OH

At the Family Reconciliation Services office of the Cuyahoga County Courthouse, on January 7, 1992, Abdulla H. Awkal, 32, allegedly opened fire with a handgun, killing Ms. Awkal and her brother. Nearby deputies seized the couple's 14 month-old child while another deputy shot and wounded Mr. Awkal.

Chicago, IL

Security guards can't even trust an innocent looking man in a wheelchair. It happened at the Richard J. Daly Center in Chicago in 1984. A man upset about a post-decree divorce proceeding with his ex-wife, smuggled a .38-caliber revolver into the courtroom under his blanket. Deputies did not ask him to go through the metal detector at the entrance to the courtroom. Once inside, he shot and killed a judge and a lawyer.

Brooklyn, NY

In March of 1993, Max Almonor, a 52-year-old parole officer, was in court because of a dispute with his wife, Danielle, about visiting privileges with their 16-year-old daughter. Mrs. Almonor was a federal parole officer. While policy calls for law enforcement officers to keep their guns and badges when in the courthouse on official business, they are supposed to give up their weapons when attending to personal affairs. Max got in the courthouse with his gun by flashing his badge.

Max and his wife passed notes to each other as they sat in the waiting room at Family Court in Brooklyn. They exchanged words before Max Almonor suddenly drew his .38-caliber service revolver and shot his wife twice in the head. She was pronounced dead at the hospital. Two by-standers were wounded, as others scrambled for safety. Shortly after the shooting, the gunman let an unarmed court officer take his weapon. He then quietly waited on a bench for police to arrive.

Bronx, New York Criminal Courts Building

A woman was fatally shot in February 1993, in the vestibule of the building, apparently in retaliation for the slayings of six people.

Dallas, TX

In January 1993, a man opened fire in a hallway of the courthouse, killing his wife and wounding a bystander before turning the gun on himself.

Poison Chocolates

Judges and their families can't even accept free gifts of chocolates unless they know who sent them. A box of Godiva chocolates, addressed to a U.S. District Court judge and his wife, were received at his home on Valentine's Day in 1987. Not suspecting anything, the judge's wife opened the box. After eating several of the poisoned chocolates she collapsed and was taken to a hospital.

Bombings

Judges, even Federal judges, now must be careful about opening any strange or unexpected packages. In a10-day period starting in December 1989, five different bombing incidents occurred. Circuit Court of Appeals Judge, Robert S. Vance was killed at his Alabama home by a package bomb. A civil rights lawyer, Robert E. Robinson was killed in his Savannah, GA home. Bombs were also sent to the 11th Circuit courthouse in Atlanta and the NAACP in Jacksonville, FL, but they were intercepted and harmed no one. A Maryland county judge was injured in a December 22, 1989, pipe-bomb explosion.

In 1992 and 1993 more letter and package bombs were sent to judges by unknown assailants. It's not an easy time for judges handling controversial cases.

FINDINGS OF THE NATIONAL SHERIFF'S ASSOCIATION

In a survey published in 1978 by the National Sheriff's Association, *Court Security: A Manual of Guidelines and Procedures,* they came across a variety of violent incidents such as:

1. A defendant kicked his court-appointed lawyer in the face and shoulders, knocking him to the floor.

2. A man involved in a civil lawsuit suddenly pulled out a gun and began shooting, killing a lawyer, and wounding the judge and a witness.

3. A violent confrontation occurred between demonstrators protesting a trial and police outside a courthouse.

4. A fire in a court building destroyed several thousand court reporter tapes of trial testimony.

5. A judge was killed by a letter bomb sent through the mail.

6. A bomb exploded in the probation department of a courthouse.

7. A sniper shot through a court window from across the street from the courthouse and killed a judge on the bench.

The Association found that the most frequent threats or incidents in courthouses involved:

- Escape or escape attempt
- Disorderly conduct

- Physical assault with a firearm or with weapon other than firearm
- Physical assault with no weapon used
- Bomb threat
- Bomb explosion
- Threat other than with a bomb
- Demonstration
- Suicide or suicide attempt
- Hostage taking situation
- Theft and fire

Source of Threats

At the time the survey was made it was found that most court violent acts, disturbances, and disruptions were caused by three kinds of people: criminals, disturbed or demented persons, and "political activists." People in these categories played different roles in a trial, such as a defendant, witness, friend or relative of either the defendant or the victim. The trial participants most likely to cause security incidents were first, defendants, and second, their friends or relatives. But at times people with no known relationship to the judicial process caused trouble.

Violence tended to occur with emotional defendants facing serious criminal charges, unhappy with their lawyers, or upset about the court proceedings. The factors stated that triggered violent behavior by defendants occurred with the revocation of bail, prosecution tactics, the judge's attitude, the presence of friends or relatives in court, and a long prison term or death sentence.

Court personnel reported to the NSA that the most dangerous people likely to cause an incident during a trial were defendants or spectators. However, they indicated that different types of trials and situations created different kinds of threats. "In gang-related cases, gang members might cause the greatest threat, while in other trials the victims or their families or friends might be the ones to cause an incident. In 'political' trials, where a cause or controversy is involved, spectators might present a greater threat than during normal criminal trials." They also believed that "revolutionaries" and juveniles were a serious threat because of their unpredictable behavior.

The Targets

The survey found that judges, lawyers, and bailiffs were the ones most in danger. In civil cases the target was likely to be the winning litigant or attorney.

NATIONAL COURT SECURITY STUDY – 1991

By 1989, court and law enforcement officials believed that due to the rising number of incidents of court violence and threats against the courts, changes were needed in courthouse security. The National Sheriff's Association found that during the period from 1979 through 1989 the "nature of court violence and the perpetrators were changing. Racial, political, and nationalist activist organizations have been employing terrorist methods of intimidation and violence: trials involving organized crime, racketeering and narcotics have presented increasingly higher risks of violence; and demonstrations to influence the courts have become commonplace in trials involving sensitive social and environmental issues." The Association began an eighteen-month study that was published in May 1991, entitled *Court Security: Training Guidelines and Curricula,* by William H. Petersen and Barbara E. Smith, Ph.D. The researchers analyzed 243 Court Security Incidents reported by courts throughout the country that had occurred during the study period.

The study found that violent incidents ranged from verbal threats to deadly assaults against judges, bailiffs, clerks, prosecutors, defense attorneys, witnesses, and spectators. The violators included the defendants,

defendants' friends and family, and unexpected sources like plaintiffs, witnesses, spectators, disgruntled court personnel, or fanatics who wanted to cause harm to the court or people in the court.

Location of Violent Incidents — Fifty-four percent of the incidents occurred in criminal courts, 11 percent in municipal courts, 11 percent in juvenile courts, eight percent in civil courts, and six percent in domestic courts.

Time and Location of Incidents — Sixty-two percent of the incidents occurred in the morning, and 38 percent in the afternoon. Forty-one percent of the incidents occurred in the courtroom, 18 percent in the court lobby, and the rest were spread around to holding cells, offices, etc.

Type of Case — Most of the incidents occurred during a criminal case, 56 percent, divorce cases, 11 percent, and juvenile offenses, eight percent. Violence took place at the time of sentence, 23 percent, arraignment, 18 percent, and trial, 13 percent.

Nature of Incidents — When an incident occurred, 56 percent assaulted someone, 23 percent disturbed the peace, seven percent attempted to flee from custody, six percent killed someone, five percent vandalized things, and three percent took a hostage.

Profile of the Perpetrators — Usually the perpetrator acted alone, 89 percent, two persons, eight percent or more than two, three percent. While most perpetrators were male, 26 percent were female.

Age of Assailant — 15 percent of the assailants were 20 or younger; 32 percent were 21-30; 32 percent were 31-40; and the remainder were over 40 years of age.

Role of Assailant in Proceedings — 74 percent were defendants, eight percent spectators, four percent plaintiffs, six percent had another role, and eight percent had no role.

Relationship to Victim — Sixty-eight percent had none; seven percent were a spouse/ex-spouse; three percent were a friend; and 22 percent had some other relationship.

Motivation of Perpetrator — Thirty-two percent were for revenge; 29 percent to escape; 30 percent to intimidate the court; eight percent to influence the court; and one percent for political reasons.

Victim's Role in Proceedings — Bailiff, 31 percent; judge, 24 percent; defendant eight percent; plaintiff, six percent; witness, five percent; prosecutor, five percent; defense attorney, three percent; spectator, two percent; and others 16 percent.

Most of the perpetrators, 68 percent, were arrested.

COURT SECURITY PLAN POLICY

Every courthouse should have a court security plan to prevent violence, a crises plan and a trauma team to cope with a violent incident if and when it should occur. As used by the National Sheriff's Association, court security means "the procedures, technology, and architectural features needed to ensure both the safety of people and property within the courthouse and nearby grounds and the integrity of the judicial process."

The authors endorse the court security policy recommendations of the National Sheriffs' Association in their manual, *Court Security* outlined below:

1. Security is needed daily, not just during special trials. Security must not be so visible that it becomes repressive.

2. One person should be responsible for overall courthouse security.

3. Prepare written court security policy statements.

4. Search the courtroom and related areas both before and after court convenes.

5. Provide adequate visitor control through directories, floor plans, receptionists, and special search operations, if necessary.

6. Prepare a contingency plan for hostage situations and special plans for high-risk trials. Also develop procedures for a fire, bomb threat, natural disaster, civil disorder, power or utility failure, or any other situation requiring a general building evacuation.

7. Provide for post event review of the response to any special situations.

8. To ensure security for judges, guard their parking spaces and assign parking by number rather than name, escort judges through public corridors, provide an alarm button in their chambers, and search chambers daily.

9. Provide private witness waiting areas if possible.

10. Give bailiffs detailed written instructions for courtroom procedures and for handling juries both under normal circumstances and when sequestered.

11. Transport in-custody defendants between jail and court by vehicle if a secure tunnel or bridge is not available.

12. When in-custody defendants are expected to present a high security risk in the courtroom, suggest additional security measures, including magnetometers at the entrances to courtrooms for the judge's approval.

13. Be aware of critical times when incidents may be expected—e.g., (1) at the appearance of an antagonistic witness or codefendant; (2) during prisoner movement between various points; (3) at arraignment and sentencing; (4) when commitment is ordered in juvenile court; (5) when a verdict is rendered in a domestic or small claims court; and (6) when unruly spectators are present.

Architectural Design of Court Facilities

If a new facility is to be built the Sheriffs' Association recommends:

1. Choose an architect with court design experience.

2. Set up separate entrances and circulation routes for incustody defendants, judges and court staff, and the public.

3. Locate public offices on lower floors in multi-story buildings, near public entrances, and away from courtrooms to reduce noise and unnecessary traffic.

4. Carefully design the prisoner reception area. Ideally, it should be a sally port, or passageway, with the entrance not visible to the public and opening directly into a secure or restricted passage.

5. Improve courtroom security through design features or duress alarms for the judge, clerk, or bailiff to summon help.

6. Design temporary holding areas to include provisions for separating prisoners, an observation port on the door of the holding room, privacy screens for toilet facilities, and any other special features needed. One or more cells can be wired for sound and CCTV for use when an unruly defendant is removed from the court.

U. S. POST OFFICES

U. S. Post Offices have suffered a number of vicious attacks that have killed 34 people and wounded 20 since 1983 and traumatized many more, in 12 post office-related shootings across the country. Two of the latest occurred within hours of each other on May 6, 1993; one in California and one in Michigan.

Dearborn, Michigan

In Dearborn, a postal mechanic, apparently angry that a female co-worker had been promoted to a clerical job he desired, walked into the Post Office garage with a handgun and a shotgun. The man, Larry Jasion, 45, opened fire on employees in the garage. One man was shot to death, a man and woman were wounded, and another man suffered chest pains and a hip injury after he fell in an attempt to escape being shot. Employees ran screaming into the street to escape. Following the shooting the wounded were hospitalized. The woman, Sandra Brandstatter, 32, was in critical condition with two gunshot wounds in the head and one in the back. The wounded man, Bruce Plumb, 43, was in stable condition with multiple gunshot wounds to the back.

Shortly after the shooting, Jasion's body was found in another part of the garage. He had killed himself with a shot to his head. The man had been an employee of the Post Office for 24 years. About six weeks before the shooting, Jasion had filed a complaint with the Equal Opportunity Commission because he had been rejected for the clerical position.

Postal Inspector Fred Van de Putte said that Jasion had been counseled about his rejection for the promotion and told how he could appeal the decision. Co-workers and authorities said that Jasion was an eccentric and embittered person. He had painted the inside of the windows of his house white so that no one could see in or out.

Officials said that after 14 people were killed by a mail carrier at an Oklahoma post office in 1986, Jasion went to his immediate supervisor and told him, "You're going to be next." The supervisor, Robert Fryz, said that he quit as garage supervisor in 1987 partly because he believed that Jasion would carry out the threat.

Dana Point, California

In December 1992, Mark Richard Hilbun was fired as a letter carrier from the Dana Point, California, Post Office partly for stalking a female co-worker. He was obsessed with Kim Springer for over a year. He had been

137

diagnosed as a manic-depressive previously. Hilbun reportedly sent Springer a letter a week before the shooting which said, "I love you. I'm going to kill us both and take us both to hell."

Witnesses and police said that Hilbun allegedly walked into the postal center through the employee entrance about 10 a.m. and yelled to workers, "Get down on the ground." He also yelled out, "Kim! Kim!" He opened fire and killed letter carrier, Charles T. Barbagallo, 42, with a shot to the head. He then shot and slightly wounded another worker who came through a door into the room. He fired through a door at the office postmaster, but didn't hit him. Kim Springer, who hid under a desk, was not hit.

Officials said that Hilbun then left the post office in a pickup truck with a kayak on top. A few blocks away he allegedly tried to rob a man working in his garage and shot him when he was unsuccessful. John Kersey, 65, who was hospitalized, reported that Hilbun approached him with a gun and said, "'This is a holdup' and put a gun to me. When I had my face on the floor he hit me over the head with the butt of a gun, I think. Then I got up and started scuffling with him." Hilbun fired several times, but Kersey was hit only once in the arm.

The police, in their search for Hilbun after the shooting, went to the Corona del Mar home of his mother, Frances Hilbun, 63, about a half an hour after the incident to obtain information about him. Neighbors told the police that they thought it was strange that they had not heard any barking from Mrs. Hilbun's dog all morning. Getting no response, the police broke open the door. They found Frances Hilbun's body in her bedroom with her dead cocker spaniel. Both of them had been stabbed many times. Police believed that Hilbun had killed his mother and her dog before he went to the post office.

Post office officials reported that one day, Hilbun arrived at work wearing his underwear outside of his uniform. When informed this was unacceptable behavior, he took it off and returned to his place of work with the underwear on top of his head wearing it like a mask.

The United States Postal Service understood the critical need to provide Hilbun with mental health assistance. Employing their internal employee assistance counselors, Hilbun was recognized quickly as a distraught and potentially violent employee. Their concerns caused the police to determine that Hilbun indeed was dangerous and placed Hilbun under psychiatric care. During this time it was reported that Hilbun made several obscene phone calls threatening the EAP counselor and his family.

It was found at this time that Hilbun was suffering from manic depression or what is now known as bipolar depression. It was the belief of the presiding psychiatrist that under medication, it would be important for Hilbun to return to work. Hilbun was scheduled to visit his psychiatrist the very day that he went on a rampage at Dana Point.

The Signs of Bipolar Depression

A manic episode of bipolar depression is a distinct period where the mood is elevated, expansive, or irritable. It can be so severe as to cause problems in occupational functioning, social gatherings, and interpersonal relationships. It may require hospitalization to prevent harm to self or others. Some of the other signs include an inflated sense of self-esteem ranging from uncritical self-confidence to marked delusional grandiosity, decreased need for sleep, loud speech, rapid and difficult to interrupt, continuous flow of accelerated speech with abrupt changes from topic to topic, sometimes disorganized and incoherent, distractibility, and an increase in goal-directed activity which involves excessive planning and participation in multiple activities. Finally, you may observe excessive involvement in pleasurable activities which may have high potential for painful consequences like foolish business investments or sexual indiscretions.

Economic Cost to the Post Office

The economic cost for violence can be staggering. Three months after the incident the shooting had cost the Postal Service over $600,000 and the costs were continuing upward.

CHURCHES/TEMPLES

California

Not even our safest institutions, like churches, are out of danger of violence.

The members of the Mt. Olive Church of God in Christ in South-Central Los Angeles learned that even their church was not a sanctuary from violence. During the Friday night service July 21, 1989, two half brothers, Albert Lewis, 37, and Anthony Oliver, 31, wearing dark clothing and ski masks planned their attack. Lewis was looking for his wife who had left him a few days earlier when she discovered that he was legally married to another woman. Unknown to Lewis at the time was the fact that his wife was hiding out in Las Vegas with her mother because Lewis had terrorized her.

Lewis stayed outside as a lookout while his half brother walked down the aisles of the church armed with a newly purchased shotgun looking for his brother's wife. He found Patronella Luke, 35, a cousin of Lewis' estranged wife, her husband Peter, and Eddie-Mae Lee, a 76-year-old family friend. Oliver opened fire killing Patronella Luke, Lee, and seriously wounded Peter Luke. The two men escaped, but were arrested several days later.

However, it wasn't until May 1993 that the trial was completed and the jury found the two men guilty of murder. The Judge, Jacqueline Connor, sentenced them to death. The *Los Angeles Times* quoted the defense attorney as saying the sentence was justified for what they had done, "If you believe in the death penalty, this case warrants it. If you go inside a church and shoot innocent people in prayer, you should be sentenced to death."

Although Lewis was not the triggerman, the jury believed that he deserved the death penalty because he was the mastermind of the murder.

Arizona

Two young men walked into the Wat Promkunaram Buddhist temple in Arizona on August 9, 1991, ransacked the monk's quarters and took $2,700 in cash, cameras, and electronic equipment. After ordering six Buddhist monks, an elderly nun, and two male followers onto the floor, Jonathan Doody systematically shot each of them to death.

On July 12, 1993, Doody, now 19, was convicted of nine counts of murder, nine of armed robbery, and one each of burglary and conspiracy to commit armed burglary. Alex Garcia, a co-defendant, who testified against Doody, pleaded guilty to first-degree murder to avoid the death penalty. Garcia claimed that he fired harmless shotgun blasts between each victim and that Doody actually killed the victims.

Doody was a military enthusiast and an avid member of his high school ROTC unit. He had told friends that he was going to the temple to test out the building's security system.

The massacre shocked the local and Thailand Asian community. Thailand's ambassador to the United States made two visits to Arizona to discuss the incident.

YOSEMITE NATIONAL PARK

While on patrol along the Tioga Pass Road at 10:15 p.m. in historic Yosemite National Park July 14, 1993,

Ranger Kim Aufhauser, 37, stopped to question a person walking along the road. The ranger got out of his car and was fired at by the man. One bullet hit his left leg and the next two shots struck his armored chest protector and did not injure him. He fell to the ground and fired three times at the fleeing person. Patrol rangers have been required to wear the bulletproof vests for some time because of increased violence. It undoubtedly save Aufhauser's life.

Unable to chase the man he radioed for help. A few hours later a hunt was underway to find the assailant. Unfortunately, the ranger could not see the person very well in the dark and did not know if it was a man or woman. This was the first shooting of a ranger and incident of this type in the 103 year history of the park. Rangers report that for several years, more people who come to the park are giving authorities problems. Park service staff were concerned because the number of rangers have been reduced 18 from the previous year due to budget constraints.

LIBRARIES

At a party in April 1993 celebrating the opening of a new $24 million library a few blocks from the Capitol in Sacramento, California, a gunman entered the festivities and without any warning, opened fire. Investigators could not determine why the bearded man, described by one witness as wearing a floppy hat and a long coat, marched into the library, went up to the third floor and opened fire, fatally wounding two victims. When library patrons and employees attending the celebration that Sunday heard the shots, they bolted for exits. One employee flagged down a passing police officer who called the SWAT team.

The gunman worked his way up a stairwell to the roof where SWAT officers cornered him on a ledge. Refusing to put his gun down after being told to do so twice, the gunman lifted his weapon and pointed it at the SWAT team. They shot him in a burst of fire, blowing the gunman off the ledge. A witness said she saw exchanges of conversation as they stood near the edge of the building and thought they were going to talk him down. But when he pointed his gun at the officers, they shot him. Two librarians, one man and one woman, were killed in the incident.

Investigators said the gunman mumbled a rambling complaint about his wife being denied the respect she deserved, but beyond that, they knew of no reason why Barrett L. Street, 38, gunned down the library employees. Street was described as a transient and part-time sculptor. He was a regular visitor to the library who had lived in the area for more than 20 years, recently in his car, and in nearby abandoned buildings.

In 1987 an arsonist set fire to the Los Angeles Central Library. When the library reopened seven years later in August 1993, the library had 100 surveillance cameras, motion detectors and access-control doors. Why? Libraries across the country are faced with increasing problems from homeless, drug abusers, and mentally ill visitors off the street The Director of the San Francisco Public Library, Rachel MacLachlan, was injured five times in 18 months, primarily from violent incidents.

Library personnel across the country have been verbally abused, physically attacked, stabbed, and shot. Many of the homeless go into libraries for shelter and are not necessarily a threat. Unfortunately, large numbers of them smell badly, bring in their bedding, and take up space needed by library users. Better care for the homeless and mentally ill could very likely reduce the problems.

LITTLE LEAGUE BASEBALL

For years some sport analysts and reporters have written of the unhealthy intensity of Little League baseball players, their families, fans, and the number of arguments and fights that occur at Little League games. The intensity went too far at a game in Castro Valley, California an upper middle-class community east of San Francisco Bay. During a seven-inning game in May 1993, the fans and players yelled taunts and racial slurs at each other and the tension went sky high.

After the game a brawl broke out. The umpire, Robert Lloyd, said that he thought he had things under control until the game ended and a 17-year-old spectator, Joseph Matteucci, was hit with a bat apparently aimed at one of the players. He died a few days later. The suspected attacker was in turn chased by three boys, hit by a rock thrown by one of the players, and taken to the hospital in serious condition.

Robert Lloyd said that the behavior of professional players — attacks on the field, trash talk, and the violence — that the young players idolize, leads them to believe such behavior is acceptable. Lloyd stated, "This whole thing happened over words. It's not only happening here in Castro Valley. It's all over the nation. We've got to come to grips with this thing."

Later someone tried to burn down the umpire's house and threw a brick through the window with a note attached with a threat, "Testify and Your [sic] Dead." Lloyd, a key witness of the violence, was threatened earlier after he identified the player who threw a rock that hit the player who allegedly killed Matteucci.

Other Little League Incidents

Some of the other Little League incidents in which players were hurt include: Whiteville, North Carolina, May 1992 — a violation of a rule requiring that all team members play resulted in a slashed throat; and Willow Springs, Illinois, August, 1990 — a change in an umpire resulted in a broken nose, fractured ribs, broken leg, and lacerated kidney. Seems like rather un-American behavior!

PART II

UNDERSTANDING HUMAN BEHAVIOR

CHAPTER 6

VIOLENCE, GUN CONTROL AND PERPETRATORS

In the Uniform Crime Report for 1991, published by the U.S. Department of Justice and the F.B.I., violent crimes reported during 1991 included more than 1.9 million offenses — the highest ever recorded. Violent crime includes four offenses, murder and non-negligent manslaughter, forcible rape, robbery, and aggravated assault. The rate was up five percent over 1990, 29 percent over 1987, and 45 percent over 1982. There were 758 violent crime offenses reported for every 100,000 persons in the U.S.

An estimated 30,000 people are killed yearly by firearms including homicides, suicides, and accidental injuries. Of the 21,505 people murdered in 1991, 14,265 were killed by guns, (11,411 by handguns), 3,405 by knives, 1,520 by clubs/blunt instruments, and 1,193 by hands, feet.

Forcible Rape — 106,593 rape offenses were reported, at a rate of 42.3 per 100,000 population. There is actually a higher number raped in the U.S. The National Women's

Study in 1991 estimated that 683,000 forcible rapes actually occurred in 1991.

Robbery — There were 687,732 offenses at a rate of 273 per 100,000 population.

At the end of 1992, more people were killed by firearms in Texas than by cars and motorcycles. Police officers are being assaulted and killed at an increasing rate. Since 1977, the first year that statistics were kept of assaults on police officers, about 49,000 were assaulted, primarily by guns and knives. By 1991, the rate was 63,000. Police officers expect to face dangerous situations, but the assaults are different now. Officers are shot at under different circumstances, while sitting in their cars, eating, or by bystanders while pursuing someone else. Police find a more violent and aggressive element exists in cities than in the past.

NATIONAL WORKPLACE VIOLENCE

Research clearly shows a significant increase in the amount of violence and conflict in the workplace in recent years. The facts indicate that traditionally dangerous types of work such as police work, bar staff, social workers, firefighters, bank tellers and others are not the only work groups at risk. As indicated in the previous chapters, even schools, hospitals, and universities have experienced violence, and lots of it. More than 7,500 cases of violent crimes were reported on the first crime reports now required annually of U.S. colleges under a new federal law. The "National Traumatic Occupational Fatalities" (NTOF) Project reported that during 1980-1985, 13 percent of all occupational fatalities were a result of homicide. The percent of on-the-job deaths that were a result of violent crime was 12 percent for males and a stunning 42 percent for females. NTOF data only reflect deaths, not injuries, trauma or other violence in the workplace.

INDUSTRY

The highest number of work related homicide deaths (36 percent) occurred in retail trade, with the services industry accounting for 17 percent of the deaths, and public administration another 11 percent. The occupational group with the highest number of work related homicides was sales workers (22 percent) with service occupation workers accounting for another 18 percent. Executives/administrators/managers accounted for 14 percent. Businesses and corporations that have seldom been concerned with workplace violence are now being confronted with this issue. Violence can erupt in situations involving an employee angry with management or from other outside clients, customers or vendors.

"Murder On The Job," a 1992 article by Peggy Stuart in **Personnel Journal,** lists 28 incidents of murder in the workplace that occurred between March 31, 1986, and November 14, 1991. In these 28 incidents, the death toll reached 161, and 56 were injured. The increase in the prevalence of the problem obviously makes one ask the haunting question: Why? What impact does this have on society? Can the reasons be identified and what can be done to prevent this growing violence?

VIOLENCE IN OTHER COUNTRIES

Violence happens in other countries as well.

Montreal, Canada

In Montreal, a university professor enraged by a dispute over tenure, returned to the school, shot and killed a fellow teacher and wounded a school administrator.

Strathfied, Australia

On August 17, 1991, an unemployed male stabbed a teenage girl to death before entering the shopping plaza with an automatic rifle killing five people and wounding eight others. He died at the scene after turning the weapon on himself.

Europe

The violent behavior of British football fans has become a national disgrace. The damage to property in Britain and other European countries runs into the multi-millions. Numerous injuries and even deaths have resulted from violent incidents during and after games. Other European country fans can be destructive during or after games. In France, a tennis fan leaned over and stabbed Monica Selles in the back with a knife because he wanted the German woman playing Selles to win. In Germany, angry anti-immigration groups have attacked foreigners and burned their homes. In Wales, people angry with Englishmen and foreigners for buying up their homes for summer use had burned down many of the houses after the owners returned to their own country. House values had dropped in value due to the weak economy.

NO ORGANIZATION IS IMMUNE

The previously mentioned incidents are a random and almost microcosmic sampling. The list of such incidents of violence in schools, hospitals, and public places grows with frightening regularity. These incidents serve to dispel at least one dangerous and common presumption: "It can't happen here." It can and does happen anywhere, at anytime, in major cities, in small towns, in private and public schools, in hospitals, college campuses, and even churches. And the perpetrators can be as psychologically diverse as Mark Hilbun, whose symptoms were as obvious as flashing neon, or outsiders who for whatever reason feel the need to express their anger with a gun.

Only a few decades ago such an outburst would have been considered unthinkable. The emotionally-enraged employee, client, student, claimant, or customer were a relatively unknown and largely ignored factor.

But as the pace of life and the style of living has accelerated and changed, fueled by a technological revolution, so have the stresses. Financial stress. Emotional stress. Family stress. Professional stress. Life suddenly has become a great deal more competitive, challenging, and daunting. And the key to keeping up in a continually more hurried society is one's job.

SOURCE OF AGGRESSION IN PEOPLE

What are the reasons behind violence in our society? Some of the best known contemporary social psychologists have looked at the problem of violence and taken the following views.

1. Kinrad Lorenz, a Nobel Prize winner in his work on animal behavior, unlike previous views that people are inherently aggressive, believes that humans will discharge aggressive behavior toward others because of a spontaneous buildup of the "aggressive instinct" in the nervous systems. Violence can be deterred through smaller acceptable ways of aggression or diverted to other channels.

2. People are culturally influenced to act in violent ways. Our society through television and cultural subgroups view aggression in positive terms. With the exception of some Latin American countries and third world nations, the United States has the highest murder rate among world nations.

Dr. Bandura takes this position a step further. The murder rate in the United States is nine times higher than most Western European nations. Bandura believes it is because aggression is modeled as an acceptable and rewarded choice. The Stanford University professor found that children are much more likely to respond aggressively as adults if they have found in the course of growing up that they are rewarded and felt successful acting in aggressive ways. In his classic experiment with children and the "bobo doll," Bandura found adult modeling of aggressive behavior will increase the child's aggressive tendencies. People learn by observing models.

3. People are frustrated because of their failure to reach their desired objectives. This study was first formulated by Yale University psychologists John Dollard, Leonard Doob, and Neal Miller. Their "frustration-aggression" hypothesis proposed in 1939 stated that all frustration produces an inclination to aggression and that every aggressive act can be traced back to some prior thwarting. Thus, the thwarted individual has the strongest urge to attack what or whoever is considered an obstacle to reaching his goal.

In some cases, this frustration may lead to displaced aggression. That is, instead of attacking the primary frustrater, the individual is most likely to attack those individuals who are associated with the primary frustrater because of physical similarity and/or have qualities similar to those possessed by the primary frustrater (value system, ethnic group, similar occupations). This may explain why John Taylor at the Orange Glen Post Office in California killed his best friend or, as in other accounts, innocent people are violently killed although they were not the primary frustrater.

It is important to remember that these views only provide a reason for the violence not an excuse for violence.

WHY SO MUCH VIOLENCE IN THE UNITED STATES?

Watching too much violence on television by children and adults is certainly suspected as a major contributor. In a study by the American Psychological Association, they estimated that the average American child, by the seventh grade, has watched 8,000 murders and 100,000 acts of violence on TV. In American cartoons, a violent act occurs on average every 90 seconds. That is 10 percent more than

10 years ago. In an article in the *New Yorker* magazine, Ken Auletta quoted the Association's report which noted the consequences of watching so many acts of violence. "Accumulated research clearly demonstrates a correlation between viewing violence and aggressive behavior – that is, heavy viewers behave more aggressively than light viewers. Children and adults who watch a large number of aggressive programs also tend to hold attitudes and values that favor the use of aggression to solve conflicts."

In a nationwide poll by the Times Mirror company in February 1993, it was found that Americans are increasingly disturbed by the violence on TV entertainment shows, and 80 percent of them believe that it's harmful to the nation. The survey showed a link between age and concern about television violence.

The majority of Americans – 72 percent of those surveyed – said that entertainment TV has too much violence, about 25 percent characterized it as a "reasonable amount" and the remainder said there is "very little" violence on TV or had no opinion.

The opinion percentages were almost the same as found by a national poll taken in 1971. What was different in the 1993 poll was that more Americans are troubled by entertainment violence now, and more believe it has a poisonous effect on society. Americans who said they were "personally bothered" by violence in TV shows jumped to 59 percent from 44 percent in 1983, with those saying they were "bothered a great deal" rising to 24 percent from 16 percent.

Eighty percent said that TV violence is "harmful" to society, compared to 64 percent in 1983. The number who think it is "very harmful" increased from 26 percent of the public to 47 percent.

Fifty-four percent said fictional TV violence was "more disturbing" than real-life TV violence. Those least concerned about TV violence were young people, non-whites, men, and lower-income groups. They were also the heaviest viewers of real-life crime-action shows.

TV VIOLENCE STUDIES

It appears that the public is close to the truth about TV violence according to recent studies. More and more social scientists, psychologists, and parents not only believe that there is too much violence on TV, but also that it is having an adverse impact on children and young people.

In seven studies undertaken in the U.S. and Canada the researchers established correlations between prolonged childhood exposure to television violence and a proclivity for physical aggressiveness that extends from pre-adolescence into adulthood. The studies were reported in *The Public Interest* quarterly in 1993 by Brandon S. Centerwall, an epidemiologist at the University of Washington.

The long-term study started when researchers heard that in 1973, a Canadian community that had not had any television was about to obtain it. This offered a great opportunity to investigate the effects of television on the community's children, and to compare their findings with two similar communities that had been exposed to television for years. The scientist first monitored the rates of inappropriate physical aggression among 45 first- and second-graders before TV was introduced. After two years of television, the rate of aggression increased 160 percent, in both boys and girls, and in both those who were aggressive to begin with and those who were not. The rate in the two communities that had television for years did not change.

Another group of researchers studied third-, fourth-, and fifth-grade boys in two Indian communities in northern Manitoba. One received television in 1973, the other in 1977. The aggressiveness of boys in the first community increased immediately, in the second it increased four years later.

Another study conducted in a semi-rural American county from 1960 to 1981 found that among persons subsequently convicted of crimes, the more television they had watched by age 8, the more serious their subsequent crimes. A "second generation effect" was that the more television a parent had watched as a child, the more severely that parent punished children. There seems to be ample evidence that abused children tend to abuse their children after becoming parents. Centerwall also studied the effect of television on violence in the prosperous industrial society of white South Africans. Because of disagreement between Afrikaner- and English-speaking South Africans, that nation had no television prior to 1975.

He studied the homicide rates among white South Africans (prior to television), white Americans, and all Canadians. From 1945 to 1974 the white homicide rate in the United States increased 93 percent, in Canada, 92 percent; in South Africa, the white homicide rate declined 7 percent.

The study found that neither civil unrest, economic growth, age distribution, urbanization, alcohol consumption, capital punishment, nor the availability of fire arms, could explain the 10-to-15 year span between the introduction of television and the doubling of the homicide rate in the U.S. and Canada — or the lag in South Africa.

Another case made by Centerwall was that the introduction of television helps explain the different rates of homicide growth for American whites and minorities. He analyzed that white households began acquiring television sets in large numbers approximately five years before minority households, probably due to income differences. White homicide rates began increasing in 1958. A parallel increase in minority homicide rates began four years later.

IMPACT OF TV VIOLENCE ON YOUNG CHILDREN

Studies show that a 14-month-old infant can adopt behavior it has seen on television. Because young children are unable to distinguish fact from fantasy, they regard television as information about how the world really works. Due to this, Centerwall claims that in the world as television presents it, violence is ubiquitous, exciting, charismatic, and effective. He believes that "In later life, serious violence is most likely to erupt at moments of severe stress—and it is precisely at such moments that adolescents and adults are most likely to revert to their earliest, most visceral sense of the role of violence in society and in personal behavior. Much of this sense will have come from television."

WHAT CAN WE DO?

Centerwall believes that violence should be treated as a public health problem and measures applied in a practical manner as is done now with nutrition and immunization. The only hope for changing the pattern of violence on television is for parents to take action. He understands why the television industry will not cooperate in reducing violence. They exist to draw audiences for advertisers. Desensitized Americans are attracted by increasingly strong doses of more graphic violence. He indicates that just a decrease of advertising revenues by one percent would cut the television industry's revenues a quarter of a billion dollars.

Americans, especially parents, must find an effective method to stop, or at least to reduce, the graphic violence on TV. Perhaps, parent and victim organizations or a new coalition of some sort should attack the problem just as Mother's Against Drunk Driving (MADD) organized to change attitudes and laws to reduce drunk driving. If millions of parents and the general public made a point of boycotting certain programs showing violence and hurt the advertising revenues of TV stations and sponsors, the authors believe they could get the message across. After all, in 1993, three of the top programs on TV; "Cheers," "Roseanne," and "Northern Exposure," were not violent type programs.

CONGRESSIONAL HEARINGS ON TV VIOLENCE

On May 12, 1993, Rep. Edward J. Markey (D-Mass), Chairman of the Telecommunications and Finance Subcommittee of the House Energy and Commerce Committee, initiated hearings to examine the depth of the problem of TV violence and its impact on children. The subcommittee was looking for potential solutions. Markey said that there was growing evidence of "a direct link between the amount of violence on American television and the amount of violence in our society."

The Representative said, "The sheer saturation of all the violent programming creates a culture of tolerance for [violence] and we just have to begin to turn it around. We can't pretend there isn't some connection." Markey advocated legislation, similar to what Centerwall recommends, that requires that all new television sets be equipped with "time-channel lock circuitry." This system enables parents to program their sets to keep their children from watching programming they deem objectionable. In addition Markey wants an industry-developed rating system on violence, similar to what is used in the motion picture rating system.

Previous attempts have been made to limit violence on TV, but have run into effective opposition by the TV industry and the courts. In the mid-1970s one solution called "family hour" sought to limit violence and restrict frank language in network programming before 9 p.m. Unfortunately, the courts struck it down.

A ray of hope shined through at the Senate hearing on television violence. On Friday May 21, 1993, television executives from ABC, CBS, NBC, Fox, and three cable networks told Congress that they weren't proud of the murderous month of programs they put on TV in their May race for ratings and assured Congress that the next season would be different.

The NBC entertainment president, Warren Littlefield, stated that, "I know that the May sweeps has gotten widespread publicity. I ask you to consider our next fall schedule." Apparently the proposed new season changes were decided after discussions with Sen. Paul Simon, D-Ill.

The executives were responding to Congress' concern and determination to quell dramatized violence or face legislative consequences. Simon is the sponsor of the TV Violence Act of 1990 which granted the TV industry an antitrust exemption to work together to calm murder and mayhem on TV. Because of the Act and pressure an unusual meeting of broadcast, cable, and motion picture executives was planned for August 2, 1993, in Los Angeles to discuss the problem.

Howard Stringer, CBS Broadcast Group president, said, "We hope that the result will be television programming that, while reflective of the society in which we live, avoids gratuitous depictions of violence that contribute nothing to our cultural life."

The Senators seemed a bit wary, however. Sen. Howard Metzenbaum, D-Ohio, warned the executives, "If you do nothing, we are going to come down harder on you than you would like us to."

Sen. Byron Dorgan, D-N.D. had previously introduced legislation during the week of discussions that would require the Federal Communications Commission to keep a 'Violence Report Card' that would list the number of violent acts on TV each quarter.

After the Television executives completed their testimony, Jack Valenti, president of the Motion Picture Assn.

of America, testified and presented a conflicting point of view. He granted that "some gratuitous violence on television should be eliminated particularly during the hours viewed by children" but insisted that "the great majority" of the most popular television programs cannot be labeled violent. Valenti said that the problem is that "we live in a violent society, born in violence, worn by violence — running through our history like a twanging scarlet wire."

Valenti's spirited defense of the industry was in contrast to the comments made by most of the TV executives.

Sen. Herb Kohl (D-WI). chairman of the Judiciary Committee's juvenile justice subcommittee, told Valenti that "the American people are going to demand that you step up and do what you must do to resolve the problem. What children see on television and in the movie houses around the country has a great impact on them."

Valenti challenged the assumptions of Simon and Kohl saying, "whether or not there is ample confirming scientific evidence that violence on a TV screen is the major villain begetting real violence in the real society can be debated."

Kerry McCluggage, chairman of Paramount Pictures Television Group, didn't seem to support Valenti's point of view and backed the Congressional committee's purpose. He said, "We share your concern for the welfare of our children. I know there is a great sense of frustration in Washington that the entertainment industry is not moving fast enough or effectively enough to address the important issues of violence on television." He added, "But there are ongoing efforts to heighten the sensitivities of the creative community to the impact and portrayal of violence, and these efforts are not merely belated responses to the threat of congressional action."

After the three-week-long hearing, it didn't appear that the head of the motion picture industry was ready to make many changes in the way movies are made. The industry certainly got the message that their actions were being watched.

During the hearings on TV violence, it was announced that a national petition drive was being formed by a new "Citizens Task Force on TV Violence." The group planned to present their petition to movie and TV industry representatives before their August, 2, 1993 meeting on the subject. Members of the task force include the National PTA, the American Medical Assn., the National Sheriff's Assn., the American Psychological Assn., the American Academy of Pediatrics, the National Council of Churches, the American Psychiatric Assn., the American Academy of Child and Adolescent Psychiatrists, the American Nurses Assn., American Academy of Nursing, and the National Assn. of Elementary School Principals.

Beverly Hilton Hotel Conference

Sponsored by the National Council for Families & Television, on August 2, 1993, the conference members of programming producers, writers and anti-violence advocates could not agree about what to do about violence or if there was really a problem. In fact, some of the TV executives wanted to know what TV violence was. Don Ohlmeyer, president of NBC, West Coast, said, "Everyone's against TV violence. I'm against TV violence. But what is it?"

There were signs that the industry was sensitive to public pressure. One producer said that networks were concerned about producing shows that carried a parental advisory label. Some networks executives confirmed that fewer crime-based TV movies were being ordered.

Sen. Paul Simon got the industry's attention in his keynote speech when he called for the formation of an Independent Advisory Office on Television Violence to develop a uniform act of standards on violence and to report on how the industry was meeting those standards. Simon gave the industry 60 days to "show some movement" in creating such a "monitoring group," or risk legislative action from Congress.

CONTROLLING GUNS

ECONOMIC COST OF SHOOTINGS

With easy access to guns and the propensity of Americans toward violence, the result is that a lot of people are killed every year by guns — about 30,000 in 1991. Thousands more are injured. What's the cost to taxpayers? The American Medical Association estimates that the yearly cost of treating gunshot wounds in the United States is $1 billion and the taxpayers pay about 85 percent of that in public hospitals. The figures don't show the physical and emotional pain, economic loss, and expenses that the victims and their families suffer.

The proliferation of guns and paying for most of the shooting aftermath **is not** a good deal for American taxpayers. The gun and ammunition manufacturers make tons of money off their sales, but the taxpayer picks up the bodies and pieces, and the tab, after the weapons have been used on humans.

How many Americans would be killed every year if guns were not available to the public? If criminals and hostile people only had hands (fists) and knives to attack people, surely, only a small percentage of the current 24,000 gun homicides would actually occur.

The five children killed in Stockton, California, schoolyard by Patrick Purdy, or the massacre of 22 people killed at Luby's Cafeteria in Killeen, Texas, would not have happened if guns were not available. It is estimated that about one-half of the households in the United States have at least one gun and that the typical gun owner is a fairly well-educated member of the middle class.

Connecticut Takes Action

In May of 1993, the Connecticut State Senate voted in favor of a bill to ban the sale of all assault weapons within the state. This a particularly important vote because Connecticut has been a center for gun manufacturing since the Revolutionary War and includes famous guns like the Colt revolver, the Remington, and the Winchester rifle.

Two other states, Virginia and New Jersey, had previously passed laws restricting the sale of handguns and banning the sale and possession of some semi-automatic weapons. Many gun control supporters, such as Handgun Control Inc., were pleased that these state votes were a setback to the National Rifle Association and could mean progress toward a more strict national gun control law.

CHANGING THE CULTURE OF VIOLENCE IN AMERICA

With the assumption that it is a worthwhile goal to reduce the violence and its aftermath in this country, what can we do? The nation can continue to arm itself and fight back against perpetrators as in the wild west days. Unfortunately, many have tried this method and evidence indicates that it is an ineffective method against gangs, surprise robberies, and attacks.

To prevent violence the following methods make more sense:

Short-term

- Provide better security of premises at schools, hospitals, institutions, and other public places.
- Train personnel in identifying potential violent employees and customers.
- Initiate bullying education and programs throughout school systems.

Long-Range Approach

- Work to ban hand gun and automatic weapons.

- Regulate the amount and time that violence that can be shown on TV.

- Create a national organization to rate violence in movies and TV programs.

- Educate parents and the public on the effect of TV violence on children and the repercussions on society.

- Approach violence as a disease that needs treatment.

Role of National Rifle Association

In the book, *Under Fire: The NRA and the Battle for Gun Control*, the author, Osha Gray Davidson, points out that the biggest pro-gun lobby's motives have changed over the years. The NRA was founded after the Civil War by a Union Army veteran who believed there was a need for better marksmanship.

After a five-year struggle Congress passed the Gun Control Act of 1968 banning the mail order sale of guns and ammunition. Davidson believes that to some in the NRA this was the first step in taking away an Americans's right to bear arms and the unraveling of the Bill of Rights. One should keep in mind that the right to bear arms was given to militiamen during the Revolutionary War in order to combat the British. It is hard to believe that our founders thought that every American needed the right to have hand guns, automatic weapons, and machine guns in their home.

While the NRA resists gun control and is often successful, Davidson points out that they don't always win. In the first six months of 1990, the NRA sent out 51.3 million pieces of mail, at a cost of about $10 million for their causes. Davidson found that between 1983 and 1988, eleven NRA-supported incumbents lost their Senate seats while no pro-gun-control incumbents lost theirs. Perhaps, the Brady Bill and groups like Handgun Control Inc., should be given more support by the public.

WHO ARE THE PERPETRATORS?

Red Flags and Warning Signs

In sketching a psychological profile of an emotionally enraged person with the potential for violence, one starting place is a review of the psychological/behavioral criteria frequently associated with individuals who become violent. Almost without fail the violent person will fall within one or more of these groups:

1. History of Violence. A history of violence is the best predictor of violence. It overshadows all others in the area of prediction. The probability of future crime increases with each prior criminal act. Whether it is a domestic history of physical and verbal abuse during adulthood, or a lifestyle of antisocial activities, such as membership in gangs, violence will usually follow unless there is treatment. Individuals who have a developmental history of violence, i.e., were abused as children, are also more likely to be violent. Violence breeds violence.

2. Psychosis. In lay language, psychosis is simply a loss of contact with reality. Psychoses include schizophrenia, major affective disorders and paranoid states. Persons with psychosis have a thought disorder that is often reflected in loose associations in their conversations, flat facial expressions and extreme ambivalence. Additionally, schizophrenics will manifest hallucinations, poor insight, verbalize and argue with their thoughts, and often express bizarre, sometimes nihilistic, delusions. For example, an individual may believe a part of his/her body is no longer present or that all the emotions and motor activity is controlled by someone else. Individuals with this disorder may even believe a UFO has landed in their backyard.

Major affective disorders may also be characterized by a loss of contact with reality, but primarily they involve a mood disorder. This disorder may be accompanied by severe depression. More will be discussed later on depression.

The paranoid or delusional disorder is the third division of psychosis. The popular concept of a paranoid is the person who is convinced that someone, perhaps even everyone, is out to get him/her. This notion is accurate as far as it goes. But there are also other manifestations of paranoia. For example, grandiose paranoids may believe they have insight that no one else has. You may see them as delusional leaders of religious cults, like Rev. Jim Jones convincing his followers to join him in a suicide pact. David Koresh and his religious followers in March 1993, caused a national sensation when they held off authorities in a shoot-out near Waco, Texas. Four federal officers were killed. Fifty-one days later most of the remaining Koresh group were burned to death by self-set fires.

The jealous and persecutory types are two other types of the paranoid disorders. Both types may resort to violence against those they believe are doing them harm. In the jealousy type, a person is irrationally convinced that his or her lover has been unfaithful. This type may demand restrictive rules in talking to the opposite sex and may follow the lover without his/her knowledge. Physically attacking the lover because of unreliable evidence is not uncommon.

The persecutory type is the most common type of the delusional disorder. These individuals have a long history of resentment toward a person or organization they feel has slighted them in the past. They will have a tendency to exaggerate the misdeeds. This person will make many attempts to "right the wrong" through legal action or harassment measures. The persecutory type must be taken seriously because they have the ability for violence.

Regardless of the paranoia, projection seems to be the primary defense mechanism of these individuals. Therefore, they will focus much of their problems and unhappiness on others, such as a supervisor. Typical clues to disturbance are:

> "I know they bug the phones around here. Joe is after me. He doesn't like me and he wants me out."

Delusions, mood swings, depression, or paranoia — their signs may be subtle or blatant. They should all be taken seriously.

3. Romance Obsession (Erotomania). This category can fall into the third division of psychosis, but the increase of this type of violence at the workplace needs to be addressed separately. What is particularly unnerving in this type of delusional disorder is that the fixated object (your employee) may be totally unaware of the high degree of attraction. This is not a sexual attraction. The erotic delusion is idealized romantic love, a bonding of almost spiritual dimensions. The fixated object may have a great deal of contact with the individual or none at all at first. Generally, the fixated object is at a higher social level, either by title, appearance, social status or financial condition. The conduct of the erotomic type is not unusual or bizarre other than this one area. Stalking, spying, visits, gifts, love letters, taping conversations, and phone calls are common.

Laura Black finally filed a temporary restraining order against Richard Farley, former co-worker and unemployed computer technician, after almost three years of romantic harassment. Farley could not stand the suffering "she had put him through" and entered his former workplace. Firing over 110 rounds of ammunition, he killed seven individuals and wounded three others. Laura Black, although wounded, survived.

The prevalence of erotomania is seen with private citizens and public celebrities. Tatiana Tarasoff, a UCLA coed, was stabbed to death after rejecting the persistent advances over time of Prosenjit Poddar. He did not want anyone else to have her. Another case of a public celebrity murder is the death of 21-year-old Becky Schaeffer, star of the situational comedy, "My Sister Sam," at the hands of an obsessive fan, Robert Bardo.

4. Chemical Dependence. Alcohol and certain drugs agitate, create paranoia and cause aggressive behavior. Although some drugs are more dangerous than others, most of them have the capacity to interfere dramatically with reasoning ability, with social inhibition, and with the ability to distinguish right from wrong. The result is that an individual who may have been marginal is pushed over the edge.

5. Depression. Depression is the most common symptom treated by counselors. Finding hope and meaning in life's darkest shadow is very difficult, sometimes impossible. Almost one in seven depressives will commit a violent act on themselves or on others up to and including suicide and/or homicide.

Signs of Depression Include:

- "I just don't care anymore. What difference does it make?" (or similar expressions of despair)
- A slowed work pace
- Perpetual blank, sad, or frowning expression
- Self-destructive behavior
- Distractibility and sluggish decision making
- Increased apathy, lack of motivation
- Withdrawing socially
- Unrealistic expectations
- Excessive self-condemnation

- Feelings of hopelessness
- Sense of helplessness
- Inappropriate guilt or shame
- Unkempt physical appearance

6. The Pathological Blamer. The external world is the reason for their problems. Those in this category accept no responsibility for their actions. Does the employee admit to wrongdoing and take responsibility for behavior or does he/she blame the organization, system or other people? "Those guys did me wrong—and they're gonna pay for it."

7. Impaired Neurological Functioning. Impaired neurological functioning reduces the capacity for impulse control. Individuals include those who were hyperactive as children, those who have brain injuries, abnormal EEGs or other subtle neurological disorders. They are more prone to aggression as they are less capable of inhibiting themselves than the average person in a similar situation.

8. Elevated Frustration with the Environment. Important outside variables to evaluate include the family environment, peer environment and job environment. A disturbance in one or more of these support systems may trigger violent behavior.

9. Interest in Weapons. When assessing an employee, student, or client regarding his/her potential for violence, ownership of a gun or gun collection, fascination with weapons, and shooting skills are significant indicators to consider. Employees or teachers should be advised to inform management of any weapon brought into the workplace or campus.

10. Personality Disorders. Personality has been defined as "consistent human behavior patterns within the individual." These patterns are lifelong and concern how we view, think about, relate to, and perceive life. Our personalities have a tremendous impact on our relationships at home or at work. When these personality patterns become inflexible, impaired, and unhealthy, the traits become disorders and can reduce effectiveness in relating to others. Two such personality disorders will be discussed because of their relationship to workplace violence.

The Antisocial Personality Disorder. Behaviorists would prefer the word "sociopath" to describe these individuals. This disorder is more common in males than females. People with this disorder tend to be irritable and aggressive with repeated track records for fighting outside the home and domestic violence inside the home. They are not opposed to harassing others, stealing, or destroying property. They have little regard for the truth, are impulsive in action, and probably own a weapon. Generally, antisocial individuals will have little remorse about wrongdoing and justify their violent behavior. Not surprisingly, the individual will not have a long-lasting, warm, and responsible relationship with family or friends. Antisocial-personality individuals will have a history of quitting jobs without having another position available, or may be unemployed for six months or more even if they were offered employment. When they are employed, it will not be unusual to have frequent absences from work without justified explanation.

Borderline Personality Disorder: The essential feature is instability and the lack of proper boundaries. You can observe the instability in interpersonal relationships, self image, and in extreme cases, self-mutilating behavior. There may be uncertainty for this individual concerning career choice, value system, long term goals, and/or sexual orientation.

This individual experiences severe mood shifts with inappropriate anger often displayed in repeated fights. Like the antisocial behavior, this person is very impulsive and can be easily irritated. Excellent manipulators of people, the borderline personality may fear a real or imagined abandonment from others. He/she is not opposed to making suicidal threats to avoid loss. The borderline-personality, much like the self-absorbed narcissistic personality, are preoccupied with self and will use people to achieve their purposes.

A Final Note: Trust your judgment and senses. Dr. Robert C. Bransfield, Associate Director of Psychiatry at the Riverview Medical Center in Red Bank, New Jersey, states, "The gut feeling that one gets when talking to people should be respected. If one feels that someone is dangerous, that person should be considered dangerous."

Based on these criteria, Mark Richard Hilbun was obvious as a potential source of danger and violence. He was an armed but as yet unexploded bomb. He fit into at least four categories—the psychotic, the severely depressed, the historically violent, and the blamer. With the addition of his unemployed status, it was only a matter of time.

VIOLENCE TAKES MANY FORMS

LEVEL ONE:

Refuses to cooperate with authority figures

Spreads rumors and gossip to harm others

Consistently argues with peers, clients

Belligerent towards peers, students

Constantly swearing at others

Unwanted sexual comments

LEVEL TWO:

Arguments increase in frequency towards students, patients/clients, vendors, co-workers and authorities or management

Refuses to obey policies and procedures

Sabotages equipment and steals property for revenge

Verbalizes wishes to hurt co-workers and/or management

Sexual or violent notes to other students, co-workers, and/or management

Sees self as victimized (me against them)

LEVEL THREE:

Frequent displays of intense anger resulting in: recurrent suicidal threats

recurrent physical fights

destroying property openly

utilizing weapons to harm others

murder, rape, and/or arson

WARNING SIGNS

Rarely in cases of violence in the workplace have warning signs been as evident as they were with Mark Richard Hilbun. In every case there is a warning sign, usually more than one, even though they're not exhibited as overtly and aggressively as in the case of Hilbun. The following list of warning signs is certain to be revised and expanded as case studies increase, but it is a good beginning, and represents reliable indicators of potential trouble for staff members and employees.

1. Attendance Problems. Falling within this category are excessive sick leave, excessive tardiness, leaving work or school early, peculiar or improbable excuses for absences, higher absentee rate than other employees and on-the-job absenteeism (leaving the worksite or school without notice).

2. Excessive Demands on Supervisor's, Teacher's, Manager's Time. Supervisors, teachers, and managers have many responsibilities including staff development. However, if the supervisor is spending an inordinate amount of time coaching or counseling the individual concerning personal problems or having to redo the individual's work, it's a signal that the individual is in need of additional assistance outside the supervisor's expertise. The role of the supervisor is to develop skills and increase productivity, not to be a counselor. Make special note if, after repeated discussion, there is no change in the individual's performance.

3. Decreased Productivity. Be aware of any individual who has had a good-to-excellent performance record in the past but recently has been struggling at work or school or making excessive mistakes because of poor judgment or inattention. Note if he/she has missed project deadlines, assignments have been late, or if he/she is wasting work time and materials. Any sudden change or pronounced deterioration in work performance should be recorded.

4. Inconsistent Work Patterns. The individual may be experiencing alternating periods of high and low productivity. Often these extremes in the quality of work are due to substance abuse and/or alcohol abuse. Monitor the different degrees of productivity to see if there is a pattern.

5. Poor on-the-Job or Peer Relationships. Several signals may be given by this warning sign. Take note of any belligerent behavior, overreaction to criticism, mood swings or verbal harassment of others.

6. Concentration Problems. A troubled individual is usually distracted and often has difficulty recalling job instructions, project details, and deadline requirements. You may see the troubled individual at his/her work station/office deep in thought about outside concerns. Often, he/she forgets badge, keys, wallet, assignments, or some other important items.

7. Safety Issues. Becoming more accident-prone is a clear indicator of stress. People under stress are apt to be reckless concerning personal safety and will disregard safety guidelines for equipment, machinery, or vehicles. They will have a tendency to take needless risks without concern to other employees' safety.

8. Poor Health and Hygiene. Marked changes in personal grooming habits are important signals to note. If a person stops wearing makeup, no longer has her hair done, wears dirty or wrinkled clothes, or if he is unshaven, when grooming was important in the past, take these warning signs of changes as warning signs of internal conflict.

9. Unusual/Changed Behavior. This can include emotional outbursts, physical violence (i.e., hitting a wall or a piece of equipment), inappropriate remarks, or vague or blatant threats. "Someone's going to pay." "This isn't right." "They'll get theirs," etc., are also signals. So are statements which might be interpreted as delusional, such as reference to UFOs, the end of the world, being spied on, seeing elves, and secretive behavior.

10. Fascination with Guns or Other Weapons. If a person talks frequently about guns and is obsessed with guns, develops skills with different weapons, likes to visit gun shops, and subscribes to gun magazines, like **Soldier of Fortune**, these behaviors, too, should be taken as indicators.

11. Evidence of Possible Drug Use or Alcohol Abuse. Secretive behavior around his/her locker, meeting other employees or visitors in remote areas, or taking long lunches may indicate substance abuse.

12. Evidence of Serious Stress in the Individual's Personal Life. Crying, excessive personal phone calls, bill collectors, recent separation, or death of a loved one.

13. Continual Excuses/Blame. Inability to accept responsibility for even the most inconsequential errors.

14. Unshakable Depression. Depressed behavior for long periods of time (low energy, little enthusiasm, cynicism or despair).

Research into incidents of violence discloses without exception the presence of at least several of these characteristics in the extremely enraged individual.

NEED FOR COMMUNICATION

Take Threats Seriously

Every school, hospital, government organization should have a clearly written policy regarding the "chain of command" for communicating ALL threats of violence, whether from an insider (student, employee) or an outsider (patient, client). Details should include what actions will be taken at all levels of management so that threats are properly evaluated and not disregarded or discounted at a lower level. The plan should detail who will be used to evaluate the situation and the credibility of the threat. Employees or students should be informed of the importance of reporting and following the established guidelines. The method of reporting should provide confidentiality for the person reporting.

It is important that principals, administrators, and senior management take seriously all comments from human resource professionals and other employees concerning potential violence. In the fast-paced, task-oriented world, administrators and managers may not be close enough to staff, employees, and students to make an accurate assessment of the immediate and long-term danger of potential violence. Human resources should be a trusted ally and important resource for valuable information.

STATE LAWS

In addition, employers should be familiar with and use state laws that prohibit certain forms of threats. Most states have laws pertaining to terroristic threats and most permit a mental examination under certain conditions. Under these laws, a person may be involuntarily hospitalized if he/she poses a danger to self or others.

ALERT AND AVERT

In addition to alerting and averting, there are even more valuable tools, and they're available to everyone at no cost. Eyes and ears. Don't just look, but see. Don't just listen, but hear. These steps can help you cope with disgruntled individuals and perhaps head off tragedy.

THE PERPETRATOR PROFILE

The typical person likely to commit murder in the public workplace, whether an insider, disgruntled employee, ex-employee, outsider, patient, student, claimant or client, is likely to give off warning signs. But unfortunately, the signs sometimes go unheeded by those who work with the person or have seen the him/her as a patient or client.

There is a demographic and psychological profile of a violent employee, patient, student, claimant, or client, and although generalization is risky, and perhaps even suspect, to some the profile of an emotionally enraged person has proven uncommonly consistent.

A potentially violent person is generally a male, although research indicates an increase in female aggression:

- Has a history of violence
- Is a loner
- Owns several guns or other weapons
- Has, in the past, requested some type of assistance
- Is an angry person with little outlet for that anger
- Has a history of interpersonal conflict
- Is often socially withdrawn and most likely has family/marital problems
- Will, after a while, stop expressing himself verbally and become introverted, whereas earlier he constantly verbalized his complaints to management and about management
- Develops symptoms of paranoia
- Exhibits self-destructive behavior

Almost without exception, the employee, staff member, patient, student, claimant, or client, who has exploded into murderous rage will fit in to some facet of this profile. This profile also can apply to the high school or college student. Usually more than one facet of the profile applies, such as with Joseph Henry, sometimes all of the above facets, such as in the case of Ybarra Torres.

COSTS TO SCHOOLS, COLLEGES, HOSPITALS AND OTHER PUBLIC ORGANIZATIONS

When violence on a campus, hospital, or workplace occurs, the cost in human terms extends far beyond the immediate loss of life. In addition to human suffering, the institution or facility will suffer many disruptions and economic costs:

- Security

- Building repair and cleanup
- Interruption of operations with students, patients, customers and clients
- Loss of productivity
- Lost work time
- Turnover of employees
- Salary continuation for those who are injured or traumatized
- Increase in workers' compensation claims
- Increase in medical claims
- Increase in insurance premium rates
- Costs of attorney fees, medical care, and psychological care for current employees.

ECONOMIC COSTS OF VIOLENCE TO ORGANIZATIONS

Dana Point Post Office

Two months after the shooting incident, post office officials estimated that the costs to handle the problems reached $600,000 and were continuing upward.

Businesses

For example, the costs to an electronic company, the Elgar Corporation, after a tragic shooting, were estimated at $400,000 in addition to those covered by insurance, and an estimated premium increase of $100,000 yearly for workers' compensation. The estimated cost to General Dynamics after an employee killed and wounded several fellow workers amounted to $1.2 million in addition to expenses covered by insurance. Twelve months after the incident, costs were still occurring.

Economic Reason for Prompt Trauma Therapy

There are sound reasons for schools, hospitals and other public organizations to provide prompt trauma therapy after a violent incident. According to statistics from Crisis Management International in a November 1991 study made by the Barrington Psychiatric Center in Los Angeles, of 200 people suffering major psychic trauma, the half that were treated soon after an incident averaged 12 weeks' recovery time before returning to work and only 13 percent chose litigation, as compared to 46 weeks' recovery time and 94 percent choosing litigation from the group that was not given immediately therapy.

CHAPTER 7

BASIC HUMAN NEEDS

THE MEANING OF WORK

Related to the ability to assist the staff and employees of schools, hospitals, and government facilities with the stresses in their lives, there is the need for a greater understanding of the value and the meaning that work has for all of us. In a sense this applies to students as well as workers because success in studies and advancement due to high grades mean a lot to serious students. Also, there are analagous opportunties for success and failure in the school environment. For example, making the football team, cheer leader team, being chosen for a school play, being accepted or rejected by peer groups. Patients and clients of organizations have the same needs to achieve and to be appreciated.

Unsurprisingly, it was Sigmund Freud who developed the first comprehensive theory about personality. The renowned psychiatrist contended that there were two primary sources of happiness and contentment in life. He identified them as:

1. The need for love. Everyone needs to have an intimate relationship with another person, or with a family unit. Without it, our feelings of significance in the world are greatly diminished.

2. The need for work. Everyone also needs to have purposeful activity that identifies his/her role in, and his/her contribution to, society.

Abraham H. Maslow, regarded as the father of humanistic psychology, is famous for his "hierarchy of human needs." He argued that human motives can be placed in an hierarchy of prominence. That is, some needs demand satisfaction before others. Maslow placed these needs in five hierarchical levels. (See Chart A.) Although there are exceptions, typically we satisfy the needs at the lower levels before becoming concerned with the needs at the higher levels.

Chart A

HIERARCHY 0F HUMAN NEEDS

SELF-ACTUALIZATION NEEDS

ESTEEM NEEDS

Admiration & respect
Perceive self as competent & achieving

BELONGINGNESS & LOVE NEEDS

Friendship & love

SAFETY NEEDS

Security, stability, structure, protection

PHYSIOLOGICAL NEEDS

Air, thirst, hunger, sleep

Food, as a physiological need, is the most basic need. Water, air, and sleep are also among the most demanding physiological priorities which must be satisfied before moving on to higher levels.

For example, if a person is hungry, his/her behavior will center on obtaining food. Until this need is met, that person will not be concerned about making new friends or developing a career. Most of us progress up the hierarchy over the course of a lifetime based on our perceptions of our relative safety, security, and belongingness in our changing life circumstances.

OTHER LEVELS OF HUMAN NEEDS:

1. Safety needs. When physiological needs are met, we become increasingly motivated by our safety needs. These include the need for security, stability, protection, freedom from fear or chaos, and the need for structure and order. These needs may become dominant when the future is murky or when the stability of the political, social or work order is threatened (witness the hoarding of food in Russia recently). Concern over the economy of a country can lead many to refrain from buying, to delay starting or adding to a family, or to take less risks at work. When people perceive a threat to their security, they will react by trying to build savings accounts, or by seeking out a job with greater security and minimal risk. They may seek out the orderliness of the military, or organized religion. People with strong safety or security needs may tend to stay in an unhappy work relationship or in an unhappy marriage.

2. Belongingness and love needs. For most of us, the need for food and water and the need for safety and stability are fairly well satisfied. It's only when our financial resources are threatened that we become concerned about our physiological and safety needs. But satisfaction of these lower-level needs does not end our quest for happiness. The need for friendship and love soon emerges. Most of us find that an exclusive devotion to producing income is unsatisfying if it means sacrificing time spent with friends and loved ones.

3. Esteem needs. Regardless of centuries of wistful poetry to the contrary, there is more to life than love, Maslow contends. Satisfaction of our need to belong and to be loved will invariably direct our attention to our need for self-esteem. The perception of oneself as competent and achieving, and receiving respect from others are the foundations of self-esteem. Satisfying these needs is not self-serving narcissism. Failure to do so results in feelings of inferiority, helplessness, and discouragement.

4. The need for self-actualization. Nearly every culture has a myth about a protagonist/hero who, by virtue of a magic lamp or contact with a supernatural being, receives everything he or she wishes. Health, wealth, love, and power. Imagine their surprise when they discover, as they inevitably do, that everything isn't enough, at least not enough to produce total happiness. Instead there's a strange new discontent and restlessness. Something's missing. That something is self-fulfillment. And so begins (for those who have satisfied their needs at the base of the pyramid), a personal quest to develop themselves to their full potential. They introspectively and repeatedly ask what they want out of life, where their lives are headed, what they want to accomplish. Many never have the opportunity to explore these questions as they become absorbed in the day-to-day fight to pay their bills and feed their families.

What Freud and Maslow have in common and with other psychologists and psychiatrists is a recognition of the value and meaning of work whether that work is perceived by the individual as a career or "just a job." In an emotionally charged and volatile time where competition for jobs is stiff, it's imperative that employers be aware of that value and meaning to their employees, particularly if they are taking it away.

Many organizations aware of the seriousness of the situation will have trained personnel, as well as trauma counselors, available on site when a lay-off is announced. The burgeoning outplacement industry in recent years is an indication of growing sensitivity to the impact which the loss of a job can have on an individual. It is not possible to measure how many potentially violent employees were averted from taking retaliatory measures because of this deliberate intervention.

STRUGGLE FOR ESTEEM

Alfred Adler believed that as weak and helpless children we are surrounded by and dependent for survival upon larger and stronger adults. The counterpoint to dependence is independence, a yearning intensified by the passage of time. First comes a desire for equality, eventually supplanted by what Adler called "humankind's need to strive for superiority."

Striving for superiority, Adler contended, was the motivating force in life. Virtually everything we do, he said, is designed to establish a sense of superiority over life's obstacles, to overcome feelings of inferiority. And the more inferior we see ourselves, the stronger our striving for superiority.

This innate drive for superiority has impact on all facets of life, including work. Adler parallels Freud in believing that work is one of only three indispensable life tasks at which every human being desires to achieve superiority. The others are the need for friends and the need to love and be loved. (See Chart B.)

Studies show that work, friends, and love affect one another and are, in fact, closely linked. For example, if we are unhappy in our job, that experience will affect our relationship with our family and our friends. A bad day at work

Chart B

WORK - ONE OF THREE LIFE TASKS

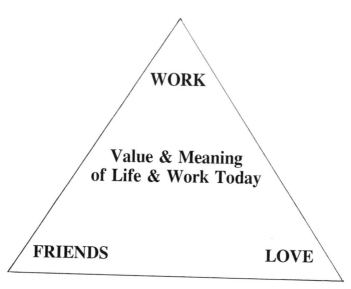

can be a harbinger of a bad night at home. It's a safe bet that even Ward Cleaver of the TV program, "Leave It To Beaver," occasionally stewed sullenly over a setback at work and was grumpy with June and the boys.

Conversely, if we are unhappy at home it will have an impact on our productivity and satisfaction at work. Personal problems, whatever they are—financial, family, marital, health—cannot be conveniently stashed in a briefcase and deposited at the door of the workplace, to be picked up at the end of the day.

STRESS INDEX

The third leg of the equilateral triangle of life's tasks is work, which has value infinitely beyond that of being a mere source of income. In contemporary society work is (perhaps unfortunately) how a person is defined. You meet a stranger at a party or at some other social gathering. After the mandatory, "How are you?" the next question is almost guaranteed to be, "What do you do?" Even more important, work is a primary source of friendships.

For many, work is a source of structure and order. It represents routine and stability in a chaotic and uncertain world. These factors compound the pain when there is a significant change, such as a termination or a layoff. The inborn sense of feeling inferior described by Adler becomes magnified, intensified, in some cases unbearably so. To compensate for the heightened feeling of inferiority, the need to strive for superiority becomes greater. For some the fastest and most accessible way to gain or regain a feeling of superiority is with a gun. So it was with Ybarra Torres (hospital shooting), Mark Hilbun (post office shooting) and many others. So it is for thousands of students and young gang members, And the list is growing. Each new tragedy forces, or should force, a painful new re-examination of the value and meaning of work or study in the case of students. Perhaps students in junior and senior high, not interested in education, should be permitted to leave so that they will not disrupt the educational goals of serious students.

UNDERSTANDING LOSS

Other factors should be considered when contemplating the value and meaning of work/school to an individual. An employee does not necessarily need to be terminated to suffer substantial loss. Loss of stature, income or opportunities, such as with a job change, or demotion, suspension from school or lack of recognition, such as with Wayne Lo at Simon's Rock College, can be just as devastating and provocative. The perception of, or actual loss of, any of the following may be a stimulus for retaliation:

1. Job Satisfaction. Some define job satisfaction as doing what you want to do. The bonus is that you get paid for it, too! Or get scholastic honors. A job that allows you to use your motivated skills and abilities in work that contributes to or enhances your ideals is satisfying. A job that allows you to maximize your capabilities is satisfying. Being transferred to a job with equal pay but tedious, unfulfilling work undercuts self-esteem and job satisfaction.

2. Growth Opportunities. Many place great value and importance on having room to grow personally and/or professionally. This doesn't necessarily mean zooming up the administration or organizational ladder. What it does mean is that the job tasks are new, challenging, and pleasant learning, experiences that stimulate growth. These same principles apply to students and the school environment as well.

3. Monetary Rewards. This does not apply to students in their younger years. Satisfaction has to come from recognition by grades or honors of some sort. For employees or staff members, many judge themselves and others by the money they earn. For them, success as a person is measured in dollars. They feel diminished if their income is reduced even a small amount. More than one university official has said that the system will go to hell if salaries are cut. At issue for them is their self-esteem. Their image of themselves is of someone who moves steadily upward in income and position, without setback. Whether compensation is satisfactory to an individual is determined not only by economic need, but frequently by what money represents. This is not a trivial consideration when compensation reductions are planned.

SELF-ESTEEM

Many employees, staff, or students driven by that innate drive for superiority, may perceive a threat to their self-esteem with the loss of any of the above. When that realization sets in, productivity and efficiency levels go down. The levels of anger and resentment go up. A dead-ended employee, an employee or student stripped of hope for advancement or betterment, is a potentially stressed person and, given the presence of other stressors, a potentially emotionally enraged person.

IDENTIFYING THE SIGNALS

There are some straightforward signals which help to identify an person who is struggling with the results of stress:

1. Disorganized Behavior. Organization and planning skills begin to suffer. The person begins to forget where he or she placed items, begins to forget important details.

2. Heightened Anxiety. Manifestations of elevated anxiety include increased body aches or headaches, changes in sleep, eating or sex patterns, changes in blood pressure, and muscle tension.

3. Personality Magnification. A fast-paced, task-oriented individual with a tendency to be aggressive and assertive becomes even more pushy and demanding. An individual with a tendency to avoid problems will continue to do so to avoid confrontation, even as resentment grows.

4. Defensive Posture. Suggestions once graciously accepted are now interpreted as browbeating. There are complaints of being "constantly used" and "picked on." Defense mechanisms often operate on a subconscious level. Thus, one may not be immediately aware of the reasons he/she is acting in particular ways.

HOW ADMINISTRATORS, MANAGERS AND SUPERVISORS CAN HELP

What does all of this mean to the supervisor who is genuinely concerned about the welfare of his/her employees or students? Or to the human resources manager concerned about the overall health and vitality of an organization who is anxious to provide sound counseling or coaching to supervisors on employee relations matters?

UNDERSTANDING THE PSYCHOLOGY OF LOSS

First, it means **understanding the psychology of job loss.** This means that any necessary "take-aways," or events that run the risk of appearing to be take-aways, should be orchestrated and planned with the same forethought and care as a major relocation, merger, or new service launch. These "take-aways" include compensation, benefits, bonuses, title, perks, special privileges, communication, vehicles, freedoms, space, opportunities, or keys. It means understanding that "loss" can include those things both material and intangible. It means understanding that, when the environment is uncertain and resources are diminished, people will hang on that much tighter to what they have, and will be that much more threatened by the potential loss of that which they value. It means **noticing** what has value to different employees under one's supervision, and knowing that what they value will differ from employee to employee.

OBSERVATION

Secondly, it means **becoming careful observers of human behavior** and becoming alert to changes in behavior — not only in the more vocal staff, employees, or students, but in those less expressive as well. It means being observant of patient and client behavior.

INTERVENTION

Third, it means **intervening to assist the staff or employee** who is exhibiting signs of being over-stressed. This assistance may not be direct. A well-timed management referral of an employee to an organization's Employee Assistance Program (EAP) or Social Services Group is frequently the most wise, practical, and efficient measure a supervisor or human resources manager can take. The EAP provides assessment, counseling, and referral by trained professionals, while the supervisor provides performance coaching, encouragement, support, and resolution of work-related problems and obstacles. The supervisor **cannot** control the behavior of an employee, but he or she does exert profound influence on the employee's immediate environment, and therefore on the employee's daily job experiences.

Clearly, not every employee who snaps at co-workers, misplaces items, expresses extreme religious or political views, or is fearful of losing his/her job is a potentially violent employee. The key point is, that in every instance of workplace violence, the emotionally enraged employee had experienced a build-up of life stresses over time. There came a point for each of them when it became simply too much to bear. The vigilant supervisor (or co-worker or family member) who moves promptly to assist the employee in alleviating those stresses, may very well save lives (even his/her own life).

RESPONSIBLITY

Does this mean that supervisors of emotionally enraged employees are to blame for their employees' actions? Absolutely not. The life/work situations leading to violent behavior are complex. Human resource specialists do not have 100 percent accurate means for predicting and preventing violence. We are all responsible, however, for educating ourselves and others to become better observers of behavior and to increase the chances of averting crises before they happen.

Unfortunately, there is no foolproof system for detecting emotionally enraged employees, students, patients, claimants, or clients, but there are guidelines, and there are warning signs. Some are subtle, some are as bright as a flare. Understanding these signs, recognizing them when they occur — and acting on that knowledge and recognition — are vital steps in heading off possible tragedy.

PART III

DEVELOPING PREVENTION AND MANAGEMENT PLANS

CHAPTER 8

SECURITY AND PREVENTION

WHY PLANS AND PROGRAMS ARE NEEDED

Human and Economic Costs

As previously mentioned, when violence occurs in the school or on college campuses, in hospitals, and government workplaces, the cost in human terms extends far beyond the immediate loss of life. In addition to the human suffering of personnel and their families, the organization itself will suffer many financial and other costs: increased security expenses, building repair and cleanup, service interruptions, productivity loss, lost work time, turnover of employees, salary continuation for those who are injured or traumatized, workers' compensation, medical claim increases and premium rate increases, attorney fees, medical costs, and psychological care for current employees. Planning can prevent human suffering and save a lot of money.

For employees or staff, the ramifications of losing a job are pervasive and cut deeply. The loss of a job (or of things of value in the work situation) is perceived as an assault on one's dignity and self-esteem. A person's security, stability, and the structure of his/her life are jeopardized.

To a student the fear of assault from fellow students or an outside intruder is disruptive of the learning environment. Teachers have the same problem. It can't be much fun teaching if you are concerned about verbal abuse, possible physical attack, or breaking up fights between students. Obviously, the daily concern about an attack from a patient affects the work of the staff of emergency rooms in hospitals. The same goes for government employees in courtrooms, public social service agencies where eligibility interviewers and social workers face much verbal and sometime physical abuse when they have to turn down applications for assistance.

These are times when materialism erodes traditional values. It's an economy that has been described as techno-Darwinian, which means the weapons have changed but only the fittest still survive. And the fittest apparently are those organizations that adhere to the five contemporary commandments of business:

- Increase revenue (organizations that are for profit)
- Save money
- Maximize production
- Cut costs
- Solve problems

The contemporary commandments of public organization are similar, but have service, not profit, as the motive (unless it is a service or hospital for profit):

- Provide quality teaching
- Provide quality service and programs to public
- Save money
- Increase efficiency of service provided
- Cut costs

- Solve problems

The bitter reality is that cutting costs today is almost automatically equated with down-sizing, and often with massive layoffs. And the ranks of the jobless — including the embittered jobless — swell.

Another reality is that solving problems rarely applies to the personal problems of the worker, who too often is considered a replaceable part. A favored argument is that no supervisor, whether responsible for a dozen workers or several dozen, has either the time or the qualifications to deal with the personal problems of his/her subordinates. The supervisor may not be able to **solve** the personal problems, but he/she is the first line of defense for **getting** the solution started. The supervisor is at least aware that such problems exist. And he/she should also be aware of what help is available to try to cope with such problems. It's infinitely better and easier to deal with a small problem before it becomes a big problem, possibly an even tragic problem.

The cost of not having a crisis management plan to cope with unforeseen events such as the Clevelend Elementary School tragedy or the Los Angeles County-USC Hospital can be high. Organizations can lessen the total impact of violent incidents by having management plans in place.

SECURITY DEVELOPMENT

One of the first steps for an organization to take to prevent violence or to cope with its aftermath is to survey their security arrangements and current services available.

1. Define the organization's assets that need protection.

An analysis should be done to determine what the organization needs to protect. Through the help of the security director (if you have one), facility engineer, facility operations manager, law enforcement agencies or a security agency, a thorough analysis of your facility should be undertaken.

You may not be able to afford all the recommendations from the professionals. However, a prioritized list will be helpful, so that you may do what is reasonable financially and culturally.

For example, installing a silent alarm button at a school office or an emergency room receptionist's desk that will immediately notify security, management, and police, is cost-effective and smart. Another is to move the receptionist behind a glass partition and locked door.

Where violence is a daily threat, double doors with a security guard at the entrance of a building, where one cannot enter without a proper access badge, may be more costly, but provide greater security.

2. Establish priorities for providing protection.

Senior management, human resources professionals, and supervisors are primary targets in incidents of workplace violence where employees or former employees are the perpetrator. Therefore determine the best location in the facilities; those that would provide the best protection, and that have a secondary exit leading away from the facility.

Receptionists are often the first to encounter an angry person and are also subject to attack. They need protection too, and their need should be given a high priority. In the case of elementary and secondary schools and colleges violence comes from a different type of perpetrator and a different kind of defense is needed than in, say, a post office. In hospitals, the emergency room staff is usually the target of violence and it is usually from a patient, not a fellow or ex-staff member. Therefore it is critical that each organization establish priorities in maintaining security.

3. Assess the organization's capability in responding quickly to institutional violence.

In order to respond effectively to a violent incident, a crisis management team must be in place. Team members should be selected in advance from departments such as Human Resources, Legal, Security, and Facility Management. Telephone numbers of the team members should be in the rolodex of every manager/supervisor. Along with the numbers of police and fire departments, the crisis management team's phone number should be on the phone for speed dialing so everyone can respond immediately.

4. Establish written policies so there is clear communication between employees and management and students and teachers concerning veiled threats.

Supervisors should be aware of their chain of command concerning potential violence of employees, and should not be viewed as hysterical or over-reactive if they mention concern about any particular employee. Corporate guidelines should be developed concerning proper responses to threats, employee harassment, warning potential victims, and notifying police. Consult labor attorneys and mental health professionals so that guidelines are legally and behaviorally sound. Make sure the written policies are followed to avoid unnecessary litigation.

5. Provide training programs and tools for pre-employment screening and for identification of potential behavioral problems.

Interview training, checking of references, and low-cost assessment tools can save the organization unnecessary pain concerning unstable employees/students. Awareness training should be provided as part of the indoctrination process as well as part of continuing in-service training. Part of supervisory training should be to keep the team aware of the warning signs of erratic behavior.

6. Make policies concerning termination.

Termination training is a must for every organization and is best handled through the human resources department. Often, improper methods are utilized by supervisors and managers in terminating an employee or expelling a student. A constant theme from angry former employees is not that they were terminated, but how they were terminated. Many could not leave with their dignity intact. Consult with an outplacement firm on proper termination procedures.

For a potentially dangerous former employee or staff member, appropriate locks should be changed. Badges, parking passes, and any company property must be returned at the time of termination.

Consider adding security personnel. Security guards can be uniformed or not, depending on what awareness level management wants their employees to have. Encourage co-workers who know the former employee to keep management advised if additional threats are made. Make note of the make and license number of former employees' automobiles.

7. Establish psychiatric resources or outplacement counseling to assist former employee.

This can provide a valuable service to the organization and to the disgruntled employee. Although confidentiality is essential in a therapeutic relationship, certain states have laws requiring that clinicians warn a person who is threatened with violence. Outplacement consultants are not under the same constraints, so their observation of the former employee during job transition can help determine for you his/her mental outlook and the likelihood of potential danger.

Once a crisis management plan has been developed, organizations should keep copies in more than one place. Many schools and government facilities have disaster plans that cover natural disasters such as earthquakes and fire which they should be able to modify to cover other kinds of violence.

DEVELOPING A MANAGEMENT PLAN

Each campus or organization needs to assess its own situation and develop policies to address a violent situation. The form the plan takes can be detailed and comprehensive, or simple and direct. There is a need to study what can be learned from past experiences. Besides **Prediction and Prevention Plans,** organizations also need to develop a **Trauma Plan** as part of positive management of violence at work. This will be discussed in a later chapter. Prediction of possible violent acts is one of the first steps to take.

PREDICTION — TYPES OF VIOLENCE

Violent incidents occur in basically four situations. First, when an employee is angry with management; second, when a student is angry with a fellow student or a teacher; third, when a patient or outside claimant or client is angry with a provider or denier of a product or service; and fourth, when a violent person from outside the organization, by chance, attacks or takes hostages. An example is the case of shooting at the library ceremony in Sacramento, California, when an outsider, Barrett L. Street, who had no known previous disagreement with the library, walked into the ceremony and killed two people.

Due to the increase in interpersonal violence, more needs to be done to predict the likelihood of violent behavior. J. Mercy and P. O'Carroll, authors of *Violence And Victims* recommend a public health approach that focuses on prevention rather than on the treatment of injury after violence has occurred. Other specialists believe that organizations can and should predict violence from insiders and outsiders. Predicting violence from outsiders is more difficult. However, even though totally accurate prediction is impossible except in extreme circumstances, employers and institutions should not ignore the potential for workplace violence. In fact, employers may be held legally accountable for **not** predicting potential violence.

Some employees or students will send warnings in much the same way suicidal persons may try to alert others as to their intentions. Employees and students contemplating violence may be troubled and disturbed by their thoughts and hope someone will intervene. While the ability to predict violence is controversial, guidelines can be established to assist management in identifying potential problems.

PREVENTION PLAN

WORKING WITH POTENTIALLY VIOLENT EMPLOYEES

James S. Cawood, author of "On the Edge: Assessing the Violent Employee" in *Security Management*, 1991, recommends taking the following actions:

STEP 1 - Develop a written plan for handling threats. It should specify that reports be made to human resources, not a manager or supervisor, because co-workers may be reluctant to report to their immediate supervisor.

STEP 2 - Make an immediate investigation by interviewing the person who reports the threat as well as any other witnesses to the incident. Gather as much information as possible about the threat and the person making it. Document this information in detail.

STEP 3 - Contact a specialist in assessing potentially violent employees to review the information and decide if further action is necessary.

STEP 4 - If an additional investigation is warranted, form a crisis management team, which includes Legal Counsel, Human Resources, and Security.

STEP 5 - Together with the specialist, develop a plan with this team. This can include a background investigation of the employee. Emphasis should be directed to locating information indicative of how the employee/student responds to stress and consideration given to the predictors of violence outlined previously. Past military service or interest in weapons should be included. The investigation must be handled discreetly to shield the organization from later claims of libel, slander, or invasion of privacy.

STEP 6 - The specialist should interview the person who reported the threat and any others who can verify or provide additional information about the employee's state of mind. This also must be done discreetly so as not to alert the suspected employee.

STEP 7 - The employee should be interviewed directly by the specialist. Provide security if it is believed the employee will become enraged. Security should be experienced and trained in handling such situations. Calm, low-key, security individuals who do not project a threatening or officious manner are recommended. Their behavior should not precipitate an incident of violence.

STEP 8 - Give the employee the rest of the day off after the interview. Give instructions that he/she is not to return to work until approval is received from a designated member of the crisis management team.

STEP 9 - The crisis management team should meet to review and analyze the information collected. If it is determined that the individual is not a threat to self or others, a decision needs to be made concerning a referral for counseling. Should this be on a voluntary basis or as a condition of employment? Should the employee be dismissed because of organization policy?

STEP 10 - If the specialist decides the individual is an immediate danger to self or others, decisions need to be made. Should mental health or law enforcement be notified? How will the employee's separation from the organization be handled? Is the organization's position defensible? Should the company seek a temporary restraining order and to what extent?

MANAGEMENT ROLE – EMPLOYEE RELATIONS & POLICIES

Management's most important line of defense in preventing workplace violence is to combine preventive human resource practices with close attention to the warning signs for the prediction of violent behavior. A plan should be in place with a management team trained on what to watch for and what procedures to follow. Decide who will evaluate the situation and lead the team and when to refer an employee for counseling.

Management must be especially alert for signs of excessive stress. Since disagreement with management has been a part of many incidents of violence, having knowledgeable, effective managers is extremely important. Frederick Ramsey, Director of the State of Maryland Employee Assistance Program, said, "The hardest thing we have to do is convince managers that you have to help people by letting them know that what they are doing is unacceptable."

EMPLOYEE ASSISTANCE PROGRAMS

Most large universities, hospitals, and government organizations have employee assistance programs (EAPs) in place. If not, such a program should be considered. Mental health services are also included in many benefit packages. These services should be available for personal and family problems as well as for on-the-job issues. Management should understand their rights as employer, and employees' rights regarding confidentiality.

EMPLOYEE, STAFF, AND STUDENT SAFETY

In-service training regarding workplace safety is an integral part of creating a safe environment. Topics can include first aid and CPR training, safety awareness, and personal safety training, as well as training in recognizing potentially violent situations in the workplace. Enhancing employee security is one way of letting employees know that management is concerned for their welfare.

School districts, administrations and employers are required by law to provide adequate security. Many court actions have raised questions of negligent security practices as well as the removal of potential hazards. Administrative controls, such as requiring that employees not work alone, and conflict resolution training are suggested. This is geared toward controlling violence from students, patients and outside clients, but can include disgruntled fellow employees.

The written plan for handling violence should include communication with security and its role in each step of the process. Details concerning what will happen before, during and after any incident should be included.

HIRING PRACTICES

Part of any plan to prevent workplace violence includes written policies concerning adequate evaluation of the people to be hired. Employers may be legally required to take measures to avoid hiring dangerous people. A tort known as *negligent hiring* obligates employers when there is an increased risk of harm by an employee toward a third party. Background investigations to determine the potential risk of hiring dangerous individuals are important.

EMPLOYEE, STAFF TERMINATIONS

In the current legal climate, sound management practices must be followed when terminations or layoffs occur. Managers must complete the required documentation and follow organization procedures or the result can be a lawsuit. Termination and layoff have been the cause of violent reactions in the past. Some general guidelines to help employers handle these delicate situations include:

- Treat all employees with respect and dignity.

- All disciplinary actions should be applied consistently to all employees/staff. If possible, stressful procedures should be avoided when an employee is pregnant, undergoing divorce, or dealing with critical illness, or the recent death of a family member.

- Have another person present when a supervisor delivers the bad news — preferably a human resources manager.

- Don't expect discharged or laid-off employees to act rationally.

- Stick to business reasons for the dismissal.

- Be confidential and be honest about the reason for the termination or layoff.

- Except in cases of fraud, theft, or other special circumstances, consider carefully the need to have security personnel present. Allow the employee to come back after-hours to clear out his/her work station.

- Have all forms and written materials regarding benefits, profit-sharing, etc. prepared in advance. Prepare a checklist of property to be accounted for.

- Spend time preparing exactly what you want to say. Be direct, concise, and businesslike.

- Change security codes and computer passwords previously used by discharged employees.

DOWNSIZING

Terminations and layoffs generate a lot of stress. Special consideration should be made when an organization is downsizing. There must be honest communication from management. Employees and staff must believe what they are told. Job stability is a major factor in people's lives and uncertainty regarding one's future employment can have a significant impact. Discuss the reasons for the reduction, allow time for questions, and be available in the future to answer additional questions.

Expect employees, staff, and teachers, in schools, to be angry. Some will be resentful and attempt to sabotage the employer or organization, or seek other forms of revenge. Security personnel should make a strong presence during this tense time. Students who believe that they have been treated unfairly, lost a scholarship, been suspended, etc., may seek revenge in a destructive manner against property and even humans.

It is recommended that employees targeted for downsizing not be notified too far in advance, except in cases requiring adherence to any State or Federal laws. This invites theft, sabotage, and loss of productivity.

If more than 25 employees are being dismissed, prepare information for the news media. Also, it is a good idea to have an organization representative call discharged employees on a regular basis until they have another job. This shows that the management still cares.

OUTPLACEMENT

Terminations due to takeovers, mergers, and downsizing are on the increase. Many employers provide outplacement services through their own human resources department or through an independent firm. Effective outplacement services are in the interest of both the employer/organization and the employee and project the image of a caring employer—both to the terminated employee and to those remaining in the organization. It is a reassuring safety net to individuals in cases of termination or downsizing. Outplacement services can be a strong factor in reducing stress and the possibility of a violent reaction from an employee.

CHAPTER 9

TRAINING PROGRAMS AND TRAUMA PLAN — AN OVERVIEW

TRAINING PROGRAM

Because of the increase in violent incidents in public workplaces, it is important for each organization to assess its individual circumstances and develop a plan of action to handle potential problems. Training will be different for each type of institution and anticipated violence, but the principles will apply to all. This plan should address **prediction** of the problem, **prevention,** which includes training of personnel to handle potentially violent situations, and the potential **trauma** of such situations. An "Alert and Avert" program for an organization must start with education. Education for all employees/staff, but particularly for managers and supervisors, can increase participants' sensitivity to the clues that suggest an employee could become dangerous. Clues that might previously have gone unnoticed or been ignored are suddenly signals to the trained observer to be on the alert, and, most importantly, to alert others.

Such training should begin with an inventory of the behaviors frequently associated with violence. Ideally, the training will not stop there. Providing a "checklist of warning signs" is only the beginning. A thorough education strategy will also deepen participants' understanding and appreciation of the meaning of work to employees. This appreciation will assist them in taking emotional/psychological precautionary steps with employees who are threatened by losses in their work and/or personal lives. Such measures, though subtle and intangible, can be as important as the company's security system.

As well as a policy to handle previously terminated or laid-off employees, a part of an overall plan to handle violent incidents should include training managers and supervisors to observe and report important warning signs of potential violent outbursts. Be aware if employees or co-workers are:

- Showing signs of lowered productivity
- Exhibiting a loss of self esteem
- Displaying a lack of job satisfaction
- In a position of no growth or opportunity
- Experiencing a major change in financial status

EDUCATION AND COMMUNICATION

The indispensable key to prevention is education and communication, perhaps beginning with communication among workers who too often dismiss as meaningless the muttered threats by fellow workers and who are reluctant to tell management for fear of ostracism. Effective communication between employees and management and personal communication between a supervisor and a potentially dangerous employee are critical. Developing communications links among departments deeply involved in anticipating and averting potential danger, such as human resources and employee assistance programs and other departments, is essential.

OPEN COMMUNICATION

Achieving open communication is an ideal, but the ideal is not easily attained. In the workplace there are five inherent barriers to complete open communications.

1. Fear. This barrier has many faces, from fear of physical injury to fear of needlessly compounding the problems of the already suspect employee, student or patient or outside client.

2. Anger. This, too, is multifaceted and applies equally to the employee's anger or the anger of the employee's supervisor at the employee's perceived ineptitude or indifference. A shouting match is not communication.

3. Denial. This is perhaps the most comfortable out, the self-delusion that maybe the problem will go away if it's ignored long enough.

4. Guilt. No rational, compassionate person wants to damage or destroy another person's life, which is an admirable trait. The rationalization, in this case misguided, goes something like this: "Well, the poor guy obviously has enough problems without me adding to them by messing up his personnel file. Anyhow, maybe part of his problem is my fault."

5. Accommodation. This is perhaps a combination of all the other barriers, the one that makes bending the rules preferable to exposing and trying to cope with the real problem. In some cases it even extends to doing the employee's work for him. In most cases it at least involves correcting and even covering up the employee's mistakes.

So, to reach the desired, even required, level of communication, the first and perhaps largest step in recognizing, identifying and, yes, helping a potentially violent employee. Barriers must be overcome. The good news is, none of those barriers is insurmountable.

MANAGEMENT RESPONSIBILITY

One thing almost all incidents of institutional violence have in common is that sometime before the emotionally enraged employee reached the breaking point and embarked on a bloody, tragic spree, he/she unfailingly exhibited telltale signs of pending trouble. In all such cases those signs went undetected, unreported, were ignored or, at best, treated lightly. Who is responsible for such glaring oversights? To narrow the field, **everybody.** There's more than enough blame to go around.

EMPLOYEE, STAFF RESPONSIBILITY

The list includes fellow employees, and in the case of schools/colleges, students. It is they who are most frequently exposed to the utterances of their enraged co-worker or fellow-student, utterances that may begin as standard gripes but eventually escalate into genuine threats, and from there into what might even be classified as self-fulfilling prophecies. When an employee says, "What happened in Edmond, Oklahoma, post office, could happen here," he has gone well beyond daily griping. It's the kind of remark that should be reported to someone higher up in the chain of command and dealt with immediately. It almost never is reported, however, for various reasons. One is the belief that it is socially unacceptable to be branded a "snitch." Another, almost as inbred, is the barrier between labor and management. A third is the American penchant for giving a person the benefit of the doubt, to dismiss such remarks with, "Well, that's just old Joe letting off steam. He really doesn't mean anything by it."

LACK OF TRAINING

Also to blame is the lack of training for supervisory personnel who are solely focused on productivity and have neither the time nor, more significantly, the inclination to take notice of an employee's personal problems. Unless, of course, those problems affect productivity, in which case the answer all too often is a summons to the employee to a closed-door meeting, during which the employee is advised to "straighten up, or else." Not exactly an enlightened approach, but still a rather basic one even today.

TRAUMA PLAN

Once an institution or organization has set policies and procedures in place to train employees, managers and supervisors to be alert and possibly predict and prevent potential violence in the workplace, the next step is to devise a trauma plan in case violence does occur.

In the midst of chaos, many important and practical decisions will need to be made. Aside from emergency medical actions and dealing with the police, innumerable problems will need attention. Examples include calming hysterical witnesses, notifying the victims' families, arranging transportation for employees, repairing phones that are inoperable, processing payroll and personnel information that may be inaccessible or destroyed, cleaning-up damaged offices and grounds, and contacting and informing the press. Management needs to take care of the practical considerations so that grieving employees can heal.

Organizations must consider how to handle the disruption to their normal activities. Classes may be cancelled, service may be delayed, someone may have to notify students, patients, and clients of changes in the schedule, etc. Having a trauma plan in place ahead of time will help an organization make it through a violent crisis.

COMPONENTS OF THE TRAUMA PLAN

Information to include in a plan is a trauma counselor who can be called to provide immediate help for distressed employees and witnesses. A person can be designated to handle the press. Details such as insurance coverage for medical expenses and transportation for employees should be addressed. Telephone teams should be set up not only to call family members on the day of the incident, but also to advise employees and their families as to available psychotherapy services, when to return to work, etc.

TRAUMA TRAINING PROGRAMS

Trauma response plans should include training programs to increase information about trauma and its psychological impact, as well as preparation of rapid response personnel to assist in crisis intervention and debriefing. They should also include procedures for monitoring individuals during emotional turmoil and recovery phases following trauma so that effective mental health referral can be made when necessary.

These plans should be proactive and include assessing an employee's potential for violence before an incident occurs, and also reactive for handling a specific crisis. The issues of privacy, labor regulations, and security should be taken into consideration.

THE ROLE OF SECURITY PERSONNEL

Immediate security decisions will have to be made. Increased security measures might include the actual presence of additional security personnel, or electronic/mechanical modifications to control physical entry and access.

POST-TRAUMATIC STRESS

In the aftermath of a violent incident, the survivors, including those who were injured, those who were targeted but missed, witnesses, co-workers, family members, and other people in the organization can be emotionally devastated and may suffer from post-traumatic stress. The event so overloads and overwhelms an individual that the psyche's normal coping mechanisms are not able to handle it. For the survivors, the workplace is no longer safe, but has become threatening.

Information on the effects and treatment of post-traumatic stress in the workplace emphasizes the importance of immediate action and early treatment in order to avoid more severe, debilitating responses at a later time. Criteria used to identify post-traumatic stress disorder are:

1. A traumatic event outside the range of ordinary human experience is experienced.

2. Persistent re-experiencing of reactions associated with the event.

3. An ongoing avoidance of trauma-related stimuli or numbing of psychological responsiveness.

4. Symptoms of increased arousal and elevated anxiety not present before the trauma event.

5. Duration of these persistent symptoms for at least one month.

Stages of Recovery

Many individuals may not reach the thresholds for a full diagnosis of Post Traumatic Stress Disorder, but may suffer a number of clinical symptoms. Individuals go through **three stages of recovery**.

The Impact Stage

Depending on the intensity and duration of the trauma, this stage may last from hours to days. Symptoms include chills, nausea, headaches, appetite disturbances, difficulty concentrating, irritability, shock, disbelief, disorientation, affective numbness, emotional suppression, depression, withdrawal, regressive behaviors, sleep disturbances, anxiety and hyper-arousal. Some may turn to increasing use of alcohol and drugs to numb their feelings.

Emotional Turmoil Stage

This stage may last several months or indefinitely. First stage symptoms continue. A wide range of changing feelings including fear, anger, grief, guilt, swings from self-confidence to self-deprecation, and frustration are experienced. A sense of lowered personal control, challenges to interpersonal trust and religious belief, an increased sense of vulnerability, loss of a sense of fairness, struggles with self-blame and an overall sense of personal violation may be experienced. Other difficulties include re-experiencing the trauma (e.g., nightmares, flashbacks, conditioned responses), an increased tendency to avoid trauma-associated stimuli and difficulty tolerating arousal.

Adjustment Stage

During this phase, the individual attempts to gain control over his or her emotional life while reformulating the meaning of the traumatic experience. To return to psychological health, the traumatic event must be processed and integrated into the individual's self-concept and world view.

PERSONAL AND ORGANIZATION LOSS

If the assimilation does not take place, the symptoms may continue and intensify. Insensitivity by the police, emergency responders, media, community agencies, or the employer can further victimize and traumatize the individual already trying to cope with the experience. If management responds slowly or with disinterest or blame, employees may experience feelings of betrayal. Survivors are at risk of ongoing stress reactions, and even rage, if management is perceived as resistant to providing information or taking corrective action.

In a situation like this, decreased productivity is a normal consequence. Time during working hours for debriefing, therapy, informal conversations among employees, and more formal group meetings is important. Management's coping with the emotional impact immediately lets employees/students know that the administration cares and is involved. When employees feel good about the employer's intervention, and that management is interested in their well-being, loyalty and goodwill toward the organization increases. Denying the severity of the incident or the need for therapy will only prolong recovery and lead to a loss of morale and perhaps lawsuits.

Whether the victim was a co-worker, family member, or student, and how directly the individual was impacted by the trauma, are other factors that influence the intensity of the trauma reaction. Pre-existing life stress, personality, management style, family support, history of prior trauma, and coping strategies will also have an effect.

In view of the stresses experienced by those involved in a violent incident in the public workplace, a well-thought out plan, informed management, and immediate response are important. Most people report losing a sense of safety and well-being. This can affect a person's entire life, including relationships with family as well as the ability to work and carry out everyday activities.

The overall goals are the decrease of distressing symptoms, the enhancement of emotional expression and the assimilation of the trauma experience for employees. The organization trauma team should provide support, reduce self-blame, restore a level of trust and strive to desensitize individuals to incapacitating fears and anxieties. The intervention may be done individually or in groups. Each situation needs careful evaluation and flexibility.

KEEP EMPLOYEES AND STAFF INFORMED

The trauma team should work with the EAP to keep employees informed. Team members should have the ability to make decisions, should be accessible 24 hours a day and be located in one place to make information dissemination convenient. The more informed and involved employees are, the better support they provide to the organization and the more comfortable they are with what has happened.

WHAT AN ORGANIZATION CAN DO

An institution or organization has several options open to them concerning intervention measures necessary to curtail and manage workplace violence.

1. Personnel Selection Procedures.

Correct personnel selection procedures are an effective way to prevent potential problems. This applies to accepting students in colleges, universities and employees with government entities.

There are two primary ways to assess future employees. The first one is through pre-employment testing. The review of research in the field indicates that workplace violence tendencies can be predicted when standardized testing instruments are used for personnel selection. Popular clinical tests such as the Minnesota Multiphasic Personality Inventory (MMPI), the California Personality Inventory (CPI), Personnel Selection Inventory (PSI) and the Sixteen Personality Factor Questionnaire (16PF) can predict aggressive behavior and potential violence.

However, certain laws within your state may prevent the use of these instruments. It would be wise to check. For example, the MMPI, a highly effective clinical instrument, has been ruled by a California court as illegal to use because of questions asking about sexual or religious beliefs. Other testing, like the 16PF, does not ask those questions and may be more acceptable in your state. The other prohibitive factor may be cost. Most of these tests require a licensed or certified mental health professional to evaluate the results. The best course of action is to check with several psychological services that provide testing to insure responsiveness and low cost.

The second effective pre-employment screening method is the interview and checking of references. An effective interview has three aspects that are equally critical in assessing a potential candidate. The first aspect is **Competency**. Most organizations have little problem assessing the competency level of the potential hire. In fact, most of the time, that is what the hiring manager is most concerned about in the interview process. However, a potentially violent employee can be very skilled.

The institution or organization hiring manager needs to spend an equal amount of time in two other areas as well: **Character** and **Chemistry**. All organizations would like to hire an individual that they can trust concerning their products and services. Integrity, authenticity, genuineness, initiative, and commitment are all by-products of one's character. Chemistry has to do with the ability to get along with others. It has been the authors' experience that most individuals fired are terminated because of interpersonal conflict. What are some of the questions that need to be asked? Ask questions that relate to work history. Probe deeply into reasons for leaving an organization and the relationship with co-workers and management. Superficial responses are not acceptable and should be a cause for alarm.

Present hypothetical situations that deal with conflict in the workplace; how does the potential employee respond? Ask the potential employee who was the most difficult person they ever worked for and why? Ask about outside interests. Be careful not to violate legal parameters. What magazines do they like to read? What was the title of the last book they read? Why did they like it? Probe with questions like why, when, where, and with whom. Checking references is critical. Although previous organizations are very reluctant to give anything but dates of employment for your potential employee, there are questions that can be asked. For example, is the individual eligible for rehire? In the case of a school, would they accept the transfer student back? Verify dates and positions. If the references do not list his or her immediate supervisor, find out why. If you are not getting positive responses to your questions, trust your instincts. Eliminating the problem at the beginning can save time, money, and even lives.

2. Supervisory Training. Supervisors should be trained to pay attention to the early warning signs of stress. Supervisors should be tuned in to staff needs. One way to be tuned in with your staff is "management by observation." Spend time walking around your site interacting with your team. Some educational and training programs recommended to enhance quality intervention are:

- Stress Management
- Effective Communication Seminars
- Conflict Resolution Seminars
- Teambuilding
- Dealing With Difficult People
- Managing Change
- Termination Training

3. On-Site Support Services. When trouble occurs, immediate response is necessary. Employee assistance professionals should be called to assist the victims. Police should immediately be notified. The first 24 hours following any traumatic incident are critical, especially concerning workplace violence. The human resource professional should contact the trauma team immediately after the incident and clear his/her calendar to meet with them. Establish a back-up communication system to reach the outside world.

4. Debriefing with Senior Management. Again, immediate action must be taken to clarify priorities, assess damage, and provide a plan of action. The trauma team needs to meet with senior managers and the human resource professionals. They need to do a comprehensive assessment of the incident and obtain a description of the participants. Vital to the trauma team are the what, when, where, how, and, if possible, the why. Such information will assist the trauma team in managing the anxiety of the employees and eventual displaced anger toward the company or key managers. They will also do an evaluation of the human resource professionals and other management personnel. It's important that there be only one communication source for the trauma team and the organization. If a human resource professional is not selected, then choose someone well known in the company for possessing strong interpersonal skills.

5. Employee, Staff, Student Debriefing. A confidential meeting within 24 hours with the employees/staff/students, a meeting that encourages an outpouring of thoughts, feelings, and behaviors of the entire organization will provide an educational perspective to the employees to help them understand the process and their future emotional responses. When lives are lost to workplace violence, the organization can never expect a return to "normal." What it must do is create a new "normal." The past should not be covered up, but it must not be dwelled upon, either.

In the wake of an incident, the college or organization will hear, loud and clear from employees, complaints about many issues management thought didn't exist. Often the employees or students will simply be expressing displaced anger because of the tragedy. However, all comments need to be heard. And it's going to require more than a suggestion box. Management must respond to employee feedback with tangible behavioral changes that will both make the employees feel management cares and make sense to the corporate goals. Often the requests are minimal in time and dollars. And they'll pay off in the long run in productivity and improved morale.

6. Individual or Group Psychotherapy. This may include family members and may take several months to several years.

7. Media Response. Expect heavy media response. It's very important that the head of the organization respond to the media. If necessary, choose a public relations/media firm to assist in the various nuances of radio and television reporting. At such a time an organization needs and wants to be seen in a positive light and heard with a sympathetic ear.

8. Flexibility. A business-as-usual attitude, even a month after a serious incident, is usually unproductive and costly. If the organization isn't flexible and understanding, even compassionate, the common result is a dramatic increase in lawsuits, disability claims, and days lost to sick leave. Additionally, there is usually a significant increase in turnover, which many organizations naively choose to view as unrelated. Turnover is costly in human and economic terms.

What kind of flexibility should be afforded the trauma team? First, latitude and privacy. Latitude in walking through the facility and interacting with the employees/students to determine potential trauma, diffuse anger, and minister to grief. Privacy in that several rooms should be reserved for the trauma team so that employees may come without fear or shame. In one case, officials provided trailers outside the facility to allow employees to have time alone.

Another effective step is providing individuals opportunities to meet in group settings with spouses, children, and others deeply involved. A clinician should always be present at such gatherings to facilitate the process. In addition, management must be sensitive to the cultural composition of its staff. One organization, aware of the many workers of Asian descent among its workforce, provided Buddhist monks to help those employees. The same organization also conducted special meetings with families because they, too, had been traumatized by the incident.

The most successful plans are those that are in place before they're needed, and procedures for dealing with trauma are no exception. Institutions and organizations need to understand that traumatic incidents in the campus, hospital, or government facility, are not limited only to violence. The loss of an employee/student through death, an injury at work, the sense of loss during downsizing are all traumatic and inflict deep psychological scars that have an impact on the organization. And always in these times the specter of violence looms increasingly large and shows no signs of diminishing.

To re-emphasize a point, every organization needs to establish a trauma team in preparation for a possible event, instead of scrambling after the tragedy has occurred. The team of counselors selected can generate good or ill feeling within an organization. Choose wisely, based on skills, credentials, and experience. Putting together a trauma team is no time to be foolishly frugal. Go after the best.

BE ALERT FOR SIGNS OF STRESS

Another vital part of the preparation process is for the human resource professional to meet with senior management to review the signs of workplace stress and signs of depression in their employees. Teaching supervisors to pay attention to the early warning signs will help attune them to the needs of their staff. Instructing them regarding proper termination procedures that are legal and empathetic is also important. They need to know what on-site support services are available to them. Debriefing with senior management ahead will speed the response time in clarifying priorities, assessing damages, and planning a course of action before an incident occurs. There is absolutely nothing embarrassing about using available outside support, but it's of paramount importance that the human resource professional actively and vigorously participate in every step of the program, and that senior management be cooperative.

As grim and depressing as the spiraling statistics on violence are, there are several measures that can be taken to reduce the possibility of tragic incidents. But there is no magic antidote for this kind of burgeoning terrorism, no foolproof formula to eliminate it entirely. It's indigenous to the times and to the human condition. So it's imperative that corporations be prepared to act instantly in the event of tragedy.

PART IV

INTERVENTIONS

CHAPTER 10

CARE-FRONTING & REINFORCEMENT

HUMAN RESOURCES

In the aftermath of a violent incident, no one takes more heat than the beleaguered professionals working in human resources. These departments are commonly overworked and understaffed. Often they don't get enough input from other departments to anticipate and perhaps avert trouble. They must cope with ever-changing, ever-expanding laws, rules and regulations regarding employment. Frequently, they are forced to deliver bad news, and may even become the potential target.

The fact is that those who work in human resources, unlike those in an employee assistance program or social services department, are not generally licensed clinical professionals. Since the workplace has become an arena for venting frustrations, often violently, human resources has been saddled with an almost unbearable burden.

If there's one thing that differentiates human resources personnel from other departments, it's probably that they are more keenly aware of the indispensable need for communication on all levels, from the mail room to the administrative or executive offices. Those in human resources eventually and invariably are called upon, sometimes too late, to deal with a "difficult" employee. Many human resources professionals have begun to recognize and appreciate the advantages of an approach called "care-fronting" in dealing with a "difficult" employee. "Care-frontation," as opposed to "confrontation," begins with the premise that any difficult employee needs **help**, not punishment, regardless of the organization's ultimate decision on how to handle the issue. It rests on the principle of respect for the worth of every individual and an unwavering belief in the value (to all concerned) of a supportive intervention.

CARE-FRONTING PRINCIPLES

There are several principles behind the "care-fronting" approach to dealing with a difficult employee. Many of them are based on familiar psychological concepts that have been around a long time. Put simply, they are:

1. Care-Fronting Targets Behavioral Issues, Not Personality Traits. If you think the difficult employee's problem stems from some basic personality characteristic, then you are likely to be pessimistic about the possibility of making any significant impact on the problem. However, if you specify the problem as something the individual is saying or doing—the behavior—then there is the basic assumption about the possibility for change. A person's behavior is malleable, changing in reaction to different circumstances. A person's behavior is visible and, therefore, can be observed and monitored.

2. Care-Fronting Views People as Developing and Changeable, Not Rigid and Inflexible. It's tempting to assume that someone you perceive as a problem person is always a problem, in all situations, with everyone, and always will be. Yet people do have a wide range of behaviors. Hopefully, the employee will be willing and able to change the undesirable behavior and become productive in **this** environment. However, if failed attempts make it impractical to continue, care-fronting assumes there is hope for the individual – if not here, then in another environment. If not now, then with time. If not with the resources immediately available, then with outside help.

3. **Care-Fronting Addresses Performance as Interactional and Situational.** It's easy to point the accusing finger at the problem person and assume that the problem is, literally, him or her. However, people behave within a certain situation and set of circumstances. Their behavior is a reaction to the situation as they perceive it. The circumstances surrounding the behavior in question are the key, both to the understanding of why someone is behaving as he/she is, and also to working out what to do about it.

It's not all their fault. Performance problems arise because of the interaction between the person and his/her environment. When there is a perceived problem with someone's behavior, the inclination is to blame the person, but blaming others doesn't solve the problem. Blaming people is also short-sighted. People behave within a context; therefore, their behavior is never the whole story. It's better to assume that the problem results from a closely intertwined mixture of variables in the person and the situation. Recognizing the interaction between the two is the necessary first step to successfully intervening.

INTERVENTION EXAMPLES

Before the specialists – in human resources, social services or in the employee assistance program – can help a troubled or difficult employee and perhaps defuse a potentially explosive situation, the troubled or difficult employee has to be identified. And that, in large part, falls to managers and supervisors. There are five steps to take in handling emotionally enraged employees, and all managers and supervisors should be aware of them:

1. Observation. The single most important thing a manager/supervisor can do to be prepared and possibly avert a serious problem early is to simply **notice** what is going on with the employees under his or her direction. This includes taking heed of changes in the employee's job performance. Paying attention to the sometimes subtle shifts in the employee's mood or relationships with others. It means not accepting unexplained dips in performance, attendance, or personal grooming, without expressing concern. It means staying close to the individual until the situation is corrected. The same principles apply to principals or deans of educational institutions and to administrators and managers of hospitals and clinics.

2. Document. Specify in writing the observable behaviors that are causing concern. Be specific and thorough with details.

Examples:

Effective Documentation - "Involved in frequent disputes with Accounting Department, uses abusive language such as 'Go to hell,' slurs his words, has an unsteady gait, giggles inappropriately. Stated to co-workers loudly that the supervisor is 'out to get him but is **he** in for a surprise.'"

Ineffective Documentation - "Hostile to others — has a bad attitude. Comes to work intoxicated. Has a personality problem — appears paranoid." This documentation is not detailed enough. These statements are conclusions. Documentation must describe the behaviors, the acts, that led to the conclusions.

Record the date, time and person(s) present. Write a detailed description of the incident in objective terms. What did you **see**? What did you **hear**? What did the individual **do**? . . . **say**? The purpose here is three-fold.

First, you will need to be specific when you talk to the employee. Second, you may need to provide data to outside helping professionals, and third, without documentation it may be difficult to justify future dismissal decisions. Moreover, documentation sharpens one's observation skills.

3. Prepare. Some in human resources and senior management or administration are gifted in presenting information without prior preparation. However, when dealing with an emotionally enraged and potentially violent individual, "flying by the seat of your pants" is not a good idea. Outline your goals in writing before the meeting listing the behavioral issues with already confirmed documented evidence. Write down the potential options and solutions to remedy the problem. Before the meeting, consult with human resources to clarify company policies and procedures. It is important that you receive their support before you meet with the employee. Rehearse with them what you will say and how you will say it. Ask them to help you anticipate possible reactions of the employee. For example, an especially impulsive and explosive employee may need to have security close by before the intervention is to begin. Prepare, prepare, and prepare. You do not want to be caught off guard! Arrange the meeting where privacy is assured. Do not discuss personality, only job performance.

4. Confront with Caring ("Care-Fronting"). Confronting an employee who is exhibiting some or all of the warning signs is an important and necessary step in preventing or averting possible violence. However, it cannot be over-emphasized that the **manner** in which this confrontation takes place can either 1) create the possibility of the individual's getting needed help **or** 2) accelerate the individual's mounting anger and make it more likely that he will become emotionally enraged. An example of how the latter can occur: A supervisor (who had done some reading about psychology and fancied himself interpersonally savvy) was faced with the task of firing one of his subordinate professional employees. After he had delivered the news, he said, "I'm sure you need to vent. Go ahead." He was surprised when the employee responded with fury. He thought he had done the right thing! Carefronting means showing a **genuine** interest and concern for what the employee is feeling. If it isn't genuine, don't do it — it won't work.

5. Follow-up. At this point, assuming you have done everything right, you have made proper behavioral observations of the employee, documented those behaviors, consulted and prepared for the intervention, and conducted the intervention in a careful, caring manner. However, this is where most people stop. The process is not over until proper follow-up procedures are followed. After the initial intervention, it is recommended that you schedule three additional meetings.

The first one should be two days after the intervention session to monitor the emotional response of the employee and clarify any points or goals set at the last meeting. The next meeting should be two weeks later in an effort to discuss improvements that have been made in job performance and areas for additional improvement. The goal continues to be encouragement and improvement. The final meeting should be one month after the initial intervention session, if warranted, with appropriate disciplinary action. Like the previous intervention, preparation and documentation are critical.

Those are the do's. There's also a paramount "don't." Don't ignore the problem. It will not go away. Just ask the people in Dearborn, Michigan.

CARE-FRONTING STEPS FOR ADMINIS-TRATORS, MANAGERS AND SUPERVISORS

1. Review the care-fronting assumptions.

a. The "problem" is behavioral, not a personality problem.

b. The employee/student has the possibility of improving, that is, changing the problem behavior.

c. The problem, at least in part, derives from the individual's life/work situation.

2. Collect the observations you've made (documented data), and review your documentation.

3. Schedule a private time and place to meet with the employee. Under certain circumstances, you may wish to have an additional person there. (For example, if you want a witness, or if you are concerned the individual may become violent in the meeting.)

4. Get straight to the point. Express the concern you have, and provide the examples from your documentation.

5. Ask the employee for his input. When the employee talks, **listen** very carefully and ensure that you've heard correctly by re-phrasing what was said. Validate his/her feelings.

6. Ask the employee what should be done about the behavior.

7. Ask how you can help.

8. Identify what specific variables in the employee, in you, and in the employee's environment are interacting to cause the behavior.

9. Identify the specific steps which you and the employee will take to support a change.

10. Set a date for a follow-up meeting to review progress.

Example

An example of how the above steps might actually take place is outlined below:

- Art is a supervisor in a government tax agency. He supervises a team of ten workers, one of whom is Milton. Art has become concerned because Milton is showing severe signs of stress and may have the potential for harming himself or others. He has noticed and documented five of the warning signs.

- **Safety Issues.** Milton had made two major errors in his work in three weeks (he'd had none in the previous 15 years).

- **Concentration Problems/Confusion.** On three occasions, Art had noticed Milton staring into space. When Art spoke to him, Milton had difficulty re-orienting himself and focusing on what Art was saying.

- **Unusual Behavior.** Milton had suddenly made frequent statements about, "Jesus speaking to him personally" about the country going to hell. He didn't seem to notice when his co-workers reacted to his statements with surprise and asked him questions. It was as if he was talking **at** them, not to them.

- **Poor Health and Hygiene.** Milton had been coming to work unkempt and with a distinct body odor.

- **Attendance Problems.** Milton had become casual and unconcerned about getting to work on time. At first he gave excuses, but then just shrugged when Art confronted him.

* * * * *

Following the steps above, Art started by:

- Reviewing the assumptions behind care-fronting. He reminded himself that Milton was not a "nut," but that he was demonstrating a change in his behavior, for which there was undoubtedly a reasonable explanation. He thought about Milton's performance in the past, which had been good, and worked to recapture the positive feelings he had once had for Milton. He resolved to make an effort to help Milton insofar as he could.

- He started documenting two weeks after he first noticed changes in Milton's behavior. He collected what he had written, supplemented from his memory, and made a list of the actual behaviors that caused him concern. He prepared a brief agenda of how he would approach Milton both before and during the meeting.

- Art approached Milton the first thing the next morning and said, "I want to talk with you at 10:00 this morning, Milton — my office will work best." Milton responded in a surly manner that if Art wanted him to meet his quota, he couldn't be sitting in meetings all day. (This said in a loud voice.) Art responded calmly, "See you at 10:00."

- During the meeting, Art begins by saying, "Milton, I'm concerned about the sudden changes I've noticed in your performance and work habits. You've been late for work, you've made a couple of major errors in your work, and you seem distracted. None of this is like you, and I am interested in what's going on with you, Milton." He then waits for Milton to respond. Milton squirms in his chair, has a pained expression, looks at the ceiling, and mumbles, "Oh, Christ." (Art does not unload all of his documentation at this point — it would be an unnecessary overkill.) He simply waits patiently for Milton to become comfortable enough to speak openly. Luckily, he eventually does. (If he had said, "Like what?" Art would have responded differently.)

- Milton talks at length about what a mess the world is in, how much he hates traffic in the morning, how he works as hard as he can but doesn't seem to get anywhere, and how he's convinced another co-worker is trying to make him look bad. Art listens without speaking, takes a note or two, and occasionally asks, "What else is bugging you?" He learns that Milton's wife has just lost her job, and that he is feeling hard pressed to pay the bills on his income alone.

Additionally, he learns that Milton's truck was broken into and the stereo stolen. Art recognizes the compounding effects that all of these seemingly unrelated stresses can have. He suspects there might be more, but this is what he has to work with. He says to Milton with genuine empathy, "Milton, you've got a lot on your plate, Buddy, I'd feel kind of off-center, too, if all that were going on in my life at once."

- Then he asks Milton what his strategy is for dealing with his problems.

- When Milton says he's not sure what he's going to do, but he has to have his job, Art suggests that he would like to call the EAP in Milton's behalf and set up an appointment. After Milton reluctantly agrees, Art asks for other ways in which he can help.

- Together, Art and Milton develop a list of the things that can be changed by Art, by Milton, and by the two of them in the work environment.

- They create an action plan for what each will do.

- They set a follow-up meeting to review progress.

CHAPTER 11

INTERVENTIONS

INTERVENTION PROCESS

Given the vagaries of human nature, there is no infallible system for identifing every potential perpetrator of violence. However, there are steps that can be taken to effectively reduce the risk of a tragic and bloody spree by an emotionally enraged employee patient or student. Prevention begins with careful observation and continual communication; the most accessible, viable and logical alternative to letting a problem fester. And, as has been pointed out repeatedly, communication involving confrontation will be more effective if it is handled with caring.

One of the more common defenses used by the school district, hospital administration, and government employers is that it's infinitely easier now to hire than to fire. Terminating an employee, particularly in a U.S. Post Office, almost routinely involves having to mollify concerned labor unions, and perhaps having to endure a lengthy series of grievance hearings.

The intervention session is difficult for both parties, like salary arbitration between a professional baseball player and the team for which he plays. It's possible things will be said, and they often are, by either or both parties that won't soon be forgotten or forgiven. The stakes in an intervention session can be much more significant than mere money. At stake can be a life, or even several lives. But as emotionally charged as these meetings may be, there are ways to make them more tolerable and successful for both sides.

INTERVENTION PRINCIPLES

A solid first step toward making an intervention session fruitful is to have a clear concept of what it is and what it isn't. What it is, or should be, is an open and frank discussion of an employee's behavior. What it isn't, or shouldn't be, is a court in which the verdict is already in. The purpose of an intervention session is not to punish the individual, but rather to help the employee get back on track, to improve and further develop the employee and, thereby, the employee's productivity. It's counterproductive and perhaps even dangerous to confront the employee in a punitive manner. The intervention session is part of the continuous development process that includes establishing clear expectations with the employee, training, coaching him/her, and regularly reviewing performance against expectations both formally and informally. The intervention is much more effective if approached from the perspective of developing and helping an individual rather than "disciplining and reprimanding."

TIPS FOR MOTIVATING BEHAVIOR CHANGE

Edward Thorndike, an American research psychologist, formulated the now famous "law of effect" in understanding how behavioral changes can be motivated. The law states, "We do and we behave to achieve those events that are reinforcing for us." As B.F. Skinner states, "The things which make us happy are the things which reinforce us." The law applies to self motivation as well as motivating others. Problem employees are not without motivation. The problem employee simply has been motivated (operant conditioning) to do the wrong things. Here are some tips for motivating individuals:

1. Clearly State the Desired Behavior so that the Person Understands the Expectations. It is very important that the employee/student clearly understands the expectations. The boundaries of appropriate and inappropriate behavior are often confusing to an emotionally upset employee.

2. Allow the Problem Individual to Present Suggestions to Achieve the Goals Desired so that there is a Personal Sense of Ownership. Making a commitment to change is very difficult, if not impossible, if the person does not provide personal ideas on how to change. A clear decision to change and expend some effort is critical. The problem individual must believe that he/she can make it happen. That is why his/her input is essential.

3. Begin With Reachable Behavioral Goals that Provide Immediate Success. The best goals, in the beginning, are small and reachable. Successful attempts at achieving the outcome will reduce the individual's anxiety and provide a history of success instead of history of failure.

4. Reward the Desired Behavior. Positive feedback, not punishment, has been found to be a more effective motivator for long term change. Punishment is only effective when the punisher is present. When the punisher leaves the office, the inappropriate behavior will resume. A classic example is driving on our freeways. Most drivers exceed the 55 mile hour speed limit while driving. However, if a police officer is on the highway, drivers slow down for fear of suffering the punishment of a traffic ticket, only to resume speeding again when the officer is out of sight.

5. Provide Immediate Reinforcement for Positive Behavior Instead of Delaying the Reward. Acknowledging the improvement as soon as possible is a powerful motivator. During this period of time, pay less attention to the failures and pay more attention to the positive strides. Verbalize your awareness of the positive change to the individual. Do not spend time on negative issues. Remember, changes take time and must be handled one step at a time.

6. Provide Consistent Regular Reinforcement as a Reward for Positive Behavior, Then Intermittent Reinforcement Over a Period of Time. Consistency is the key. In the first few weeks, regular reinforcement of positive behavior needs to be given and all follow-up of positive behavior needs to be acknowledged at all follow up meetings. Provide more follow up meetings at the beginning, then cut back over time. Once the new behavior has been modeled fairly consistently, then providing occasional reinforcement will be most effective.

7. Provide Social Reinforcement as a Reward for Positive Behavior. Monetary reward has its place as a positive reinforcer, especially for those who are in lower salary ranges. Money may not be as effective for senior level management or administration whose salaries exceed basic living expenses. Obviously, there are exceptions. One of the most powerful reinforcement tools is social. Affirmation, recognition, acceptance, and appreciation in words and deeds help the troubled person build self-esteem and encourage positive behavior at the workplace.

8. Model the Desired Positive Behavior. It is important that the walk matches the talk. Most individuals are very sensitive to the incongruence between management's perspective of how work and social interaction is to be conducted and how management practices do or do not live up to those standards.

No one said there wasn't a lot of effort involved in trying to alleviate a potentially volatile situation. But the rewards for such effort are immeasurable, not only in what is accomplished — getting a life back on track — but also in what is averted — tragedy in the workplace.

THE ROLE OF THE ORGANIZATION

Every organization has the same problem and the same asset: people. Although the primary mission of any organization is productivity through education and/or service, the means to achieve those goals are imperfect. Once an individual is hired by an organization, a psychological bond has been created. The employer expects loyalty. In exchange, the employee receives compensation. Inferred in this agreement by the employee is security. The feeling is, "If I do my job correctly, I will be here." Unfortunately, as we know, that is not true. Downsizing and budget cuts have reminded us painfully that personal performance is not a guarantee of security.

One of the significant changes that has occurred in our society during the last twenty years is in the family support system. When personal problems mount, it is not unusual for employees to look for support outside of work primarily with their family. Today family support is lacking for many. This is particularly true for the potentially violent employee with a history of fragmented interpersonal relationships. Much of their identity is tied to their vocation and they look at their company as a surrogate family during times of need. This places teachers, the human resources professional, supervisors, administrators, and management in the role of a skilled helper. The employee's cry for help is also a statement of trust, and the organization can provide significant assistance to the employee even in a crisis situation.

Here are some suggestions to follow during a crisis:

1. Remain Calm, Kind, and Actively Present. Your elevated anxiety will only add to an already tense atmosphere created by the employee. Be relaxed, natural and comfortable. Face the employee squarely and maintain good eye contact. Adopt an open posture and occasionally lean toward the employee while you are listening. Listen with your eyes observing the non-verbal signals such as facial expression, bodily behavior, general appearance, and autonomic psychological responses. Focus on the person first, not the problem.

2. Gather Information. Identifing and clarifying the immediate problem is critical. Ask questions and allow the employee to tell you the story. Focus primarily on the who, what, when, where, and how, type of questions. Asking why questions at this stage is inappropriate. Examples of some questions are:

- When did this happen?
- Tell me what happened.
- How did you respond?
- What is the present situation?
- Where were you at the time?

3. Assess the Information. After you have gathered information about the specific experiences, actions taken, feelings conveyed, and current status, determine what is important to the employee. Look for core messages and themes in the information provided. Assess what is important to the employee and what he/she wants you to understand.

4. Clarify and Identify What the Employee Defines as Helpful. Identify exactly what the employee would like you to do. Sometimes it is clear-cut, at other times you will need to probe. Clarify and prioritize the needs. Repeat back to the employee what you feel he/she is requesting of you. Look for confirmation.

5. Select Resources. There are many things you can do to assist your employee. However, realizing your limitations is the key to your success. Perhaps the crisis demands assistance from a mental health professional, or a police officer. Other times the resources can be family members or friends. If your organization has an EAP or social services program, make that number readily available or have the number of several clinicians in your area who can respond quickly. If you believe outside resources are not needed, keep the employees' agenda in focus. Develop a bias toward action and behavioral goals. Do not judge the individual or coerce him/her toward some action.

6. Communicate Organization Benefits. Many employees are unaware of all the benefits within the organization. Information about counseling assistance, emergency leaves of absence, insurance coverage for medical or psychological care, chemical dependency programs or a number of other services needs to be conveyed to assist the employee. A well informed management team can save a valuable employee much unnecessary stress.

LEVEL OF DANGER

Any intervention procedures must be balanced with a realization that the employee may be dangerous. It is important to review the profile and warning signs of a potentially violent individual before the intervention. Personal safety must be your primary focus.

ENCOUNTERING AN ANGRY PATIENT/CLIENT

Along with the increase in violence in the workplace by a current or former employee, there is also significant increase in violence by patients, students, claimants, clients or other outsiders. Many organizations provide services to the public where routine visits are made by the customer to the places of employment to make payments or register complaints. In many instances a violent situation develops. What can the employee do when facing potentially violent clients or claimants?

The following steps are recommended:

1. Observe. When there is any outward sign of intoxication, hallucinations, unusual or bizarre speech, security should be called immediately. Any type of positive intervention at this point would be fruitless. Simply listen to the complaint until assistance arrives.

2. Listen. The patient/client needs to know you are willing to help them. They need to feel that it is your top priority to solve their particular problem.

3. Avoid Defensiveness. A patient/client may complain about the quality of service he/she received and you may be, unfortunately, the only representative to whom they are able to air their grievance. To avoid escalation, do not defend the actions of your organization. There may be excellent reasons why specific actions were taken, but this is not the time to provide a defense. The goal is to "hear" the complaint without placing responsibility back on the patient/client.

4. Acknowledge Their Emotion Through Support. This will reduce the client's or patient's fear and hostility. They are expecting a confrontation. Do not provide fuel for their emotion. For example, it would be appropriate to say, "I would like to help. Let's see how we can resolve the problem," or "I can understand how you would be upset, please tell me how we can help you."

5. Avoid An Audience. If there are many clients or patients in the same room, take the angry individual to a private setting. This will serve two purposes, one, the irate person will feel he/she is receiving special attention, and secondly, you will be able to avoid the psychological ripple effect of agitating others who may be on the edge.

6. Establish Boundaries. The individual may make comments to you that have nothing to do with the problem. Calling you inappropriate names is a form of violence. At first, ignore any comments that do not have to do with the problem. Reduce the person's anxiety by keeping to the subject. Explain to the person what you need to assist the individual with his/her problem. At no time would it be appropriate to lash back.

7. Speak Slowly, Softly, and Clearly. Slow down your pattern of speech to reduce the individual's anxiety. Usually the angry person is talking very fast and his/her entire body is in the fight/flight mode. When you begin to slow down your speech, you will find the individual will begin to slow down as well. This effect will reduce the elevated anxiety.

8. Ask Questions. There is tremendous power in asking questions. The other person is doing the majority of the talking, yet you are in control. Ask questions that are relevant to the problem, and respond by repeating their answer so they know they are being understood. For example: "Mr. Jones, I can understand why you feel angry. How can we best help you? May I offer some suggestions to solve this problem?"

9. State Consequences. If the individual remains belligerent, step away for a few minutes to regain control and solicit additional help. This may provide the person some time to calm down and allow you to consult with another employee concerning this situation. If the person persists with threats, inform the individual that you will notify security unless he or she calms down. Employees such as receptionists, teachers, admitting room personnel, managers, and supervisors, who are in situations where they may be the first to encounter an outraged client, customer, or fellow employee, should be trained in self-protection. These protective measures can help reduce the tension of the distraught individual.

ADDITIONAL GUIDELINES

- Do not allow the person to sit between you and the door. You must have the ability to exit first and fast.

- Remain seated two to three arms length away. This provides adequate distance from the upset person yet provides for effective communication. Don't turn your back.

- Do not have any scissors or other sharp objects on your desk during the intervention.

- If possible, have a second party in the room that is your opposite sex. Often, for example, two males can create a "macho" type atmosphere unwittingly fighting for verbal territory and power. A third party (in this case, female) can provide another alternative or solution to the impasse.

- If you feel you are in danger, security should be alerted as well as human resources.

PLAN FOR PROTECTION

1. Establish policies for handling potentially violent situations.

2. Secure a pre-arranged distress signal.

3. Establish conditions and procedures for calling security, county mental health emergency team, and/or police.

4. Outline procedures for notifying employee assistance providers, social services departments and medical assistance.

5. Develop a list of potentially violent persons.

6. Provide training for all staff concerning possible trauma incidents.

PART V

CONCLUSION

CHAPTER 12

SUMMARY OF PLANS TO PREVENT VIOLENCE

ACTION BY INDIVIDUALS AND GROUPS

As can be seen, much needs to be done to prevent and control violence: promote gun control, stop bullying in schools, reduce TV violence, improve security in places of education and public places, and respond in a more positive manner to the needs of employees, students, patients, and clients.

Some of the necessary action to reach desirable goals will take federal and state legislation. The nation's legislators need the courage to ban the unauthorized use of hand guns and assault weapons. Existing and future victim organizations need to raise the consiousness of the public to problems and needs, and keep the legislators' feet to the fire.

Every person can do something. Parents can monitor their children's schools and colleges to ensure they are taking adequate security measures. Each parent should ensure that their child is not a problem to others, and that school authorities establish a good learning environment that's safe and secure.

Educators should prevent bullying in their schools, and establish workable alternative teaching facilities for problem students.

Administrators and managers should establish better employee hiring procedures, and provide more skills-training and support for their employees.

Become part of an existing organization and fight for more control of guns or for less TV violence. But join in and help bring about needed changes.

ACTION BY ORGANIZATIONS

Due to the increase in violence in institutions, it is wise for every organization to have a Violence Prevention and Management Plan in place. Each school, college, hospital, and government agency should evaluate its physical security policies, its crisis management policies, and develop a plan for preventing and managing potential violence from employees and/or outsiders.

Sound plans include training to identify potential perpetrators, and to instruct managers, supervisors, and workers to follow administrative procedures. Open communication between management and employees should be encouraged. Detailed instructions for handling the aftermath of a violent incident and the ensuing trauma and chaos are included. The following are steps to be taken in the prediction, prevention, and management of violence in the public workplace.

PREDICTION

Managers, administrators, teachers, supervisors, and workers should be trained to identify the profile of potential perpetrators, to recognize individuals under stress. Sound management procedures for hiring, downsizing, or terminations should be followed. Administrators, managers and supervisors should be taught to observe employee behavior for any warning signs. Workers should be taught to report any threats or indications of potential violence.

COMPONENTS

1. Conduct training to identify potential sources of violence. Familiarize employees with the profile of potential violent perpetrators.

2. Train employees to be alert to warning signs and to avert violence by reporting any threatening remarks or situations.

3. Train employees and management to observe — to know the basic levels of human needs and how to recognize stress.

4. Conduct training of managers/supervisors on hiring, downsizing and termination procedures.

5. If not already in existence, consider establishing an employee assistance program (EAP).

SECURITY PLAN and POLICIES

While there is no 100 percent reliable prevention program, the effort to train managers, supervisors and employees to identify potentially violent individuals and to practice open communication is well worth the effort. Many incidents described in this book could have been avoided if threats had been taken seriously. Taking preventive steps will also save the organization money by lowering the costs of lost productivity, damage to institution image, employee turnover, increased insurance premiums, and potential litigation.

COMPONENTS

1. Define the organization's assets that need protection.

2. Establish priorities for providing protection.

3. Develop sound physical security plan/systems — Identify any problem areas — Have written security procedures.

4. Assess the organization's capability to respond quickly to workplace violence.

5. Establish written policies so there are clear lines of communication between employees and management concerning veiled threats.

6. Provide training programs and tools for adequate pre-employment screening and potential behavioral problems.

7. Establish written policies concerning terminated or laid-off employees, or when "downsizing."

8. Establish psychiatric resources or outplacement services for former employees.

9. Train managers and supervisors to use Care-fronting and Intervention procedures when dealing with employees.

10. Train all employees in methods of self-protection, both verbal and non-verbal.

TRAUMA PLAN

Just as it is wise for organizations to establish management plans to deal with natural disasters, so too it is important to have a trauma plan in place to deal with the chaos of a violent incident in the workplace. Myriad decisions have to be made concerning security, employee reactions, medical emergencies and law enforcement. With a plan in place, the organization is forearmed for such an occurrence.

COMPONENTS

1. Form a Crisis Management Team with individuals from Human Resources, Legal, Security, Social Services and other departments.

This team should include:

- Security personnel to handle immediate security needs such as evacuation or closing of the building.
- Emergency medical procedures — Who to contact, etc.
- Emergency law enforcement procedures — Who to contact, etc.
- A professional trauma counselor.

2. Establish a telephone team from Human Resources to call family members and to notify employees of when to return to work, where to find help, etc.

3. Establish a second source of communication, if possible, in case the telephone system should be destroyed.

4. Establish a plan to provide information about trauma and post traumatic stress. Employees should be kept well informed on what the organization is doing to help after a violent incident.

Trauma Plans, identifying all responsible individuals, should be provided to management and kept in more than one place. Important phone numbers should be made available to all administrators, managers, supervisors, and appropriate employees.

SUMMARY

While no one likes to accept the fact that violence is increasing in the workplace of public institutions, many organizations recognize the necessity of establishing sound prevention and management plans to offset the potential danger and expense of violent incidents. Hopefully, these plans will help prevent disasters in the public workplace and ease healing in cases where a tragedy does occur. Well thought out plans allow an organization, its employees, patients, students, or clients to return to a healthy and productive workplace if violence occurs. The interaction among senior management, human resource professionals, and a psychological trauma team will assist in rebuilding the goals and vision of the organization.

PART VI

APPENDIX/RESOURCES

APPENDIX I.

PHYSICAL SECURITY PLAN FOR SCHOOLS AND COLLEGES

The following criteria and outline of security concerns may be used in planning for physical safety in schools and colleges. Original source: National School Safety Center and Little Rock, AR, School District.

The guidelines below should be followed for exterior doors or for interior doors where security is important.

DOORS

1. Locking hardware should be in working order.

2. The framework should be strong and the door fit snugly.

3. Strike plate should be strong and securely fixed.

4. There should be no breakable glass (in door or sidelights) within 10 inches of panic bar or button.

5. Insure that the door cannot be bypassed (through transom or decorative paneling above door).

6. Make sure the panic bar operates properly.

7. Make sure that exposed hinge-pins or outswing doors cannot be easily removed.

8. Secure the inactive (stationary) leaf on double doors at both the top and bottom.

9. Secure overhead door with auxiliary locking device.

10. Remove key numbers from all padlocks.

11. Equip exterior doors with panic bar and secure with heavy-duty chain and padlock at night and on weekends.

WINDOWS

The below criteria should be followed for all ground floor windows.

1. The locking hardware should be in good working order.

2. Openings should be protected with burglar resistant plexiglas or decorative grill.

3. Window openings with air conditioning units should have additional security.

4. Basement windows should be protected with security grill or well cover.

Other Openings And Outbuildings

Any openings and exterior barriers should be checked for adequate wood skids. Pallets and boxes should be kept away from rear security. Particular attention should be given to outbuildings, roof-hatches, cornices above porches, and sheds containing combustibles or expensive maintenance or athletic equipment.

CONTROL OF KEYS

The below criteria should be followed for controlling important keys:

1. Responsibility for lock and key control should be assigned to a single individual.

2. File Keys and duplicates should be kept in a steel key cabinet under lock and key.

3. All keys should be maintained and issued with strict supervision, including the requirement that each key issued must be signed for (using key receipt tags).

4. Master keys should be kept to a minimum and are retained by top administrative personnel only (principal, assistant principal, and maintenance supervisor).

5. Appropriate penalties should be made when an employee loses a key.

6. Keys should be collected from employees who terminate or transfer.

7. All keys should be collected and logged at the conclusion of the school year; the key control system should be re-evaluated, inadequacies corrected before keys are reissued.

8. Tumblers in vital locks should be changed if keys are permanently lost or stolen.

LIGHTING AND ELECTRICAL BOXES

The below criteria should be followed for lighting and electrical boxes.

1. All lights should be checked periodically for proper operation.

2. Repairs to lights and replacement of inoperative lamps should be made immediately.

3. Photo electric cells should be located out of reach of spotlights.

4. Lighting should be provided at entrances and other points of possible intrusion.

5. Switches and controls should be properly located and protected.

6. Materials and equipment in storage areas should be properly arranged to provide adequate lighting.

7. Corridors and stairwells should be properly lighted for safety.

8. Directional lights should be aimed at the building rather than away from it.

PERIMETER AND GROUNDS

Fencing - Check to insure that:

1. The fencing is high enough.

2. All trees and telephone poles are far enough away.

3. Gates are well constructed.

4. Gates are secured by good padlocks or chains.

Landscaping - Check to insure that:

1. Shrubs adjacent to the building are trimmed low enough.

2. Perimeter trees and shrubs permit patrol visibility.

3. Wood skids, pallets, or boxes are kept away from rear doors and windows.

4. Vacant lots or buildings adjacent to school grounds are kept neat.

5. School grounds and landscape are kept free of loose rocks, gravel, stones, and bricks.

6. Dumpsters are kept far enough from building to prevent window or roof access.

Visibility and Access - Check to insure that:

1. All areas of the school buildings and grounds are accessible to cruising police vehicles.

2. Buildings are visible to passing patrol cars.

ACCESS CONTROL PROCEDURES

Visitors - Insure that:

1. Written regulations are prepared regarding the access and control of visitors to the school.

2. All visitors should be greeted upon entering the school.

3. One entrance is designed for visitors.

4. Signs at other entrances requesting visitors to use only the designated entrance.

5. Visitors are required to sign in.

6. Visitors are issued identification cards or badges.

7. Proper identification is required of vendors, salespersons, and repairmen.

8. Deliveries are made at one entrance designated for this purpose.

9. Suspicious persons observed loitering on school grounds are reported to the police.

Students - Insure that:

1. There are written regulations restricting student access to school grounds and buildings.

2. Restricted areas are properly identified.

3. Students are required to carry a pass when exempted from attendance of classes.

4. Students are restricted from loitering in corridors, hallways, and restrooms.

5. Students are restricted from entering the vacant classrooms alone.

6. Parents, relatives, or friends are required to have written permission to pick up a student from school during or after school hours.

Staff - Insure that:

1. Staff members who remain after school hours are required to sign in/out.

2. Faculty members are required to lock classrooms upon leaving.

3. One person is designated to perform the following security checks at the end of each school day.

- Check that all classrooms are locked.
- Check all restrooms, locker-rooms to assure that no one is hiding.
- Check all exterior entrances to assure that they are locked.
- Check all night lights to assure that they have been turned on.
- Check the alarm system to assure that it is functioning properly.

4. Signs restricting access to school grounds are posted.

5. Walls and fixtures in unsupervised hand-out areas are durable and well protected.

PROPERTY IDENTIFICATION AND INVENTORY CONTROL

1. All school equipment should be marked permanently with school property number.

2. Items not inventoried should be properly marked.

3. An up-to-date inventory of all school equipment should be maintained.

4. A perpetual inventory should be maintained for all expendable school supplies.

ALARMS

Insure that the school is protected by an alarm system and that:

1. There is a test of the entire system at least every six months.

2. The number of false alarms are kept below two for any six-month period.

3. Upon alarm activation there should be a trained technician on the site within ten minutes.

4. Responsible members of the community living near the school should be requested to call the police if the alarm bell is heard.

5. There is always someone available with keys to the school and alarm when the alarm is activated.

6. Suitable procedures are established for turning the system on and off.

7. High-risk areas are protected (i.e. Office, Cafeteria, Shops, Laboratories, Music Rooms, etc.).

8. If public utility power fails, there should be back-up power to keep the system operating without generating an alarm signal.

GENERAL SCHOOL SECURITY

1. Students should not be allowed to carry large book bags from class to class.

2. A written plan for student supervision should be on file in the principal's office.

3. All emergency drills should be practiced regularly.

- Fire drills/Bomb drills
- Earthquake drills/Tornado drills
- Reverse fire drills/Gunman drills

4. Written records of all drills should be kept in the office.

5. Lockers should be checked for weapons on a regular basis. A written plan for weapon checks should be on file in the principal's office.

6. Shrubbery on the campus should be neatly trimmed.

7. All classroom doors should be left uncovered, affording visibility into classrooms (if doors have window glass).

8. Graffiti should be removed immediately and not left on walls.

9. Convex mirrors should be installed at blind spots in buildings.

10. Classroom and perimeter doors should be locked during school hours.

11. Signs should be posted on campus directing visitors to report to the office.

12. All classrooms should have a working intercom.

13. There should be adequate exterior lighting around buildings.

14. A club is available for students to help foster an appreciation for crime prevention.

15. School uses available resources to ensure that students may report school crimes without fear of being named in reports, suspensions, etc.

16. Employees have received inservice on personal security while at school.

17. School money is kept locked in school vault or deposited with the bookkeeper.

18. School money is counted in a place where students and the public cannot view proceedings.

19. The school Crisis Management Team meets regularly to discuss problems and concerns.

20. The principal and staff have developed a School Emergency Plan and the plan is kept where it is easily available in the event of an emergency.

APPENDIX II

College Security Questionnaire For Parents and Students: To be Completed by Campus Police Department

---

INSTITUTION   DATE

CAMPUS OFFICIAL   TITLE

■ Please provide information regarding campus crime during the past 3 years, stating how many felonies were reported on campus and resulted in convictions, in each of the following categories:

	Reported	Convicted
Number of homicides......................		
Number of sexual assaults..............		
Number of robberies........................		
Number of assaults.........................		
Number of burglaries.......................		
Number of criminal trespasses........		
Number of liquor violations..............		
Number of drug violations...............		
Number of weapon violations...........		

■ Is this information regularly disseminated to parents and students each year?....❑Yes ❑No

■ How many campus police and security personnel are currently in your employ? _____.

■ How many campus police are on active patrol during each working shift? _____.

■ How many students live on campus? _____.

■ What is the ratio of students to campus police and security personnel? _____.

PLEASE ANSWER THE FOLLOWING QUESTIONS:

1. Do dormitories have security personnel stationed at entrances on a 24-hour basis?.........❑Yes ❑No

2. Is a registration log kept of non-resident guests entering dormitories on a 24-hour basis? ....❑Yes ❑No

3. Are security personnel professionals or semi-trained students? (circle one)

4. Do police and security personnel conduct regular foot patrols of the campus?.........❑Yes ❑No

- Page One -

264

- Questionnaire (Continued) -

5. Do police and security personnel enter and patrol hallways of dormitories?.......❏Yes ❏No

6. Do all dormitory doors lock automatically?..... ❏Yes ❏No

7. Do dormitory doors have electronic alarms to warn of propped doors?...... ❏Yes ❏No

8. Are single sex dormitories available to all students upon request?..... ❏Yes ❏No

9. Does your application for admission ask students about prior felony convictions?..... ❏Yes ❏No

10. Are prospective students tested during their physical exams for the presence of alcohol and other drugs? .... ❏Yes ❏No

11. Are students expelled for drug use on campus?..... ❏Yes ❏No

12. Are under-age state liquor laws vigorously enforced by campus police?..... ❏Yes ❏No

13. Can a dormitory resident promptly arrange for a different roommate or room if their present roommate is engaged in illegal activities or using drugs in the dorm room?..... ❏Yes ❏No

14. Which administrator do students petition if a student encounters the problem(s) mentioned in the preceding question? (Name/Title)_____.

Additional questions or comments:

Please complete and return to the applicant:

_____

(Student's Name)

_____

(Address)

Prepared by: Security on Campus Inc. and Sponsored by the National Victim Center - 1 (800) FYI-CALL

APPENDIX III

SPECIFIC PROVISIONS OF THE BILL

1. The *educational component of the bill* requires personnel to receive at minimum continuing education relating to personal safety, safety and self-defense techniques, and postincident training. The bill requires that personnel receive this education within 1 year of the bill's enactment. We still have to establish credentialing for instructors qualified to teach the programs and a core curriculum of course content.

2. The second portion of the bill deals with *structural changes* within the emergency department. We are amending state law to allow the Joint Commission on the Accreditation of Healthcare Organizations (JCAHO) or state surveyors to be charged with conducting an assessment of each hospital's need for additional security measures during each accreditation survey. These recommendations will be based on the number of reported incidents of aggression or acts of violence at each hospital, potential for aggression or violence because of the hospital's location, patient population, previous episodes of aggression or violence, input from hospital staff, and law enforcement reports. Hospitals will be required to develop a format for reporting incidents of aggression or violence. Hospitals or administrators found guilty of willfully failing to provide information or who provide false information will be subject to a $25,000 fine. On the basis of the survey, hospitals may be required to institute security measures, including but not limited to metal detectors, surveillance cameras, limiting access to the emergency department for the public, installing bullet-proof glass at designated areas, installing emergency "panic" buttons to activate local law enforcement, and assignment of security personnel to the emergency department. Hospitals will be required to implement JCAHO's survey recommendations within 2 years of the survey. Failure to comply with the recommendations would result in a $25,000 fine assessed every 6 months until all recommendations have been complied with.

3. The third component relates to *security officer minimum training*, equipment, and enforcement standards. The bill states that hospital security services will be required within 2 years to have all security officers complete and obtain certification in basic security officer training, as outlined by the International Association of Hospital Security and Safety (IAHSS). Security officers are to be equipped with sufficient nonlethal equipment to respond adequately to aggressive or violent behavior.

4. Finally, because it was believed that some facilities downplayed the issue of violence or were concerned that reporting of violent acts would cause public relations problems, the bill includes provisions for *mandatory crime reporting* and prosecution. Any act of aggression or violence directed toward any ED personnel is to be reported to local law enforcement officers within 24 hours of occurrence. Any individual interfering with or obstructing the reporting process would be guilty of a misdemeanor and subject to criminal prosecution (with a minimum jail term of 6 months) and/or fine not to exceed $25,000. If sufficient evidence is present to warrant prosecution, local prosecutors are obligated to proceed with criminal proceedings against perpetrators of violent crimes. Acts of aggression or violence will be tried according to respective sections in the California penal code.

Summary

We hope that by introducing this bill emergency nurses will make a statement to the public that violence in the emergency department will not be tolerated. We also hope that with this article and information other states will be able to draft and introduce similar legislation to protect themselves. If you wish information on how to introduce legislation, please feel free to contact the authors through the ENA National Office.

APPENDIX IV

Figure 1

EMERGENCY DEPARTMENT PUBLIC SAFETY SURVEY PROCEDURES

I. Administration

1. All individuals applying for a position in the emergency department should undergo pre-employment screening for:
   a. Assurance that they can handle stress
   b. Assurance that they can effectively deal with people
   c. Assurance of proper licensing
   d. Honesty

2. All individuals employed by the emergency department should undergo a comprehensive background check.

II. Visitor control

1. All visitors, including employees not having official business, should check in at the triage desk before entering the emergency department.

2. Visitor passes should be issued before entry is made and should be:
   a. Distinctive by color, shape, or other design
   b. Date validated or self-destructive
   c. Easily displayed
   d. Collected prior to departure from the department

3. Doors between the emergency room and triage should be kept closed at all times to help simplify access control.

4. No more than two visitors per patient should be allowed in the department at any time, without prior approval of appropriate staff.

5. All visitors should enter/exit the emergency department via the main entrance near triage.

III. Access/Egress control

1. All non-treatment areas, with doors, should be kept closed and locked whenever vacant.

2. The ~~south and west~~ doors to the emergency department should be equipped with card access.

3. A "buzz-in" system should be installed on the main entrance to the emergency department to prevent unauthorized access.

4. Visitors should not be allowed to wander throughout the hospital after visiting hours. Vending machines should be installed in the waiting room to discourage wandering.

5. Members of the media/press should be denied access to treatment areas and waiting rooms.

6. The confidentiality of patients should be protected.

IV. Alarm systems

1. The cashier area, triage desk, and nurses station should be equipped with a "panic alarm" for ease in contacting the public safety department and/or the local police.

2. Portable, carry-along transmitters should be added to the system to enable nursing personnel to contact the public safety department and/or the local police.

3. Alarms should be checked monthly to ensure they are operating properly.

V. Closed circuit television

1. A closed circuit television (CCTV) camera should be installed near the emergency room entrance.

2. A CCTV camera should be installed in the "quiet room" and monitored at the nurses station.

3. The CCTV system should be checked monthly to ensure proper function.

VI. Employee training

1. All employees, including emergency room physicians, should be provided with security orientation training specific to the emergency department with special attention to:
   a. Management of violent behavior
   b. Robbery response
   c. Use of alarms
   d. Use of restraints

e. Proper ways to contact public safety or the local police
f. Performance of visual checks of patients and visitors to identify potentially dangerous persons
g. Narcotics diversion

2. Security awareness should be updated annually.

VII. Supplies

1. All supplies received from the pharmacy and/or materials management department should be visually inspected and counted for verification of receipt.

2. All supplies received should immediately be locked in a secure area upon verification.

3. No supplies should be directly delivered to the emergency department from outside the hospital, except in the case of extreme urgency.

4. Supplies issued to other departments and/or ambulance personnel should be signed for by the receiver.

5. A list of all supplies and equipment should be maintained and should include:
   a. Type of equipment
   b. Serial number
   c. Value (purchase price)
   d. Place of purchase

6. Supplies should be periodically inventoried.

VIII. High security risk patients

1. High risk patients should be placed in a special high security room. (A "quiet room.") This room should be equipped with:
   a. Shatterproof lighting
   b. Solid ceilings
   c. Outside light switches
   d. Plexiglas window with screen
   e. Low-profile security alarms

In addition, this room should not have any blind corners or visual obstructions and no sharp instruments of any kind stored inside. The room should be closed and locked when not in use. Immediately after a person is released, the room should be cleaned and inspected.

2. High security risk patients include, but are not limited to:
   a. Patients in police custody
   b. Victims of violent crime
   c. Patients involved in fights
   d. Overdose patients
   e. Suicidal patients
   f. Gang members
   g. Known criminals/previous offenders
   h. Intoxicated/impaired patients (AOA)
   i. Psychiatric patients

IX. Miscellaneous

1. Emergency department staff should immediately report the loss of keys and identification cards to their department manager and the public safety department.

2. All thefts and/or losses should be reported to the public safety department as soon as they are discovered.

3. All carts in the emergency room treatment areas should be equipped with safety straps for unruly patients.

4. An adequate number of leather restraints should be kept in the emergency department for immediate access as necessary.

5. A policy needs to be established to address the expectations of the nursing, public safety departments, etc. for patients choosing to leave against medical advice (AMA).

6. Waiting room furnishings should be permanently attached to the floor to prevent their being used as weapons.

7. A "threat assessment" should be done at least annually by a competent security professional. (This service is available through the public safety department.) The assessment should include:
   a. Everything listed above
   b. Any additions, deletions, or changes made during the year

8. A policy should be established to ensure that the procedures herein are adhered to.

Source: South Suburban Hospital, Hazel Crest, IL.

RESOURCES

CRISIS ASSISTANCE

Scripps Center for Quality Management, Inc.
(Crisis Solution Division)
S. Anthony Baron, Ph.D., Psy.D.
9747 Business Park Ave.
San Diego, CA 92131
(619) 566-3472, (619) 450-6226

Crisis Management Group, Inc.
Echo Bridge Office Park
377 Elliot St.
Newton Upper Falls, MA 02164
(617) 969-7600
(800) 444-7262

Crime Victims Research and Treatment Center
Medical University of South Carolina
171 Ashley Ave.
Charleston, SC 29425
(803) 792-2945

Crisis Management International
Norman E. Shockley
3399 Peachtree Rd., N.E.
The Lenox Building, Suite 1470
Atlanta, GA 30326
(800) 274-7470

Riverside Crisis Team
Mark Braverman
190 Lenox St.
Norwood, MA 02062

American Society for Industrial Security
1655 North Fort Myer Dr.
Arlington, VA 22209
(703) 522-5800

NATIONAL PSYCHOLOGICAL ASSOCIATIONS

American Psychological Association
750 1st St., NE
Washington, DC 20006

American Association for Marriage and Family Therapy
1100 17th St., NW, 10th Floor
Washington, DC 20036
(202) 452-0109

Society of Human Resources Management
HR Magazine—Crisis Management Checklist
606 N. Washington St.
Alexandria, VA 22314
(703) 548-3440

NATIONAL VICTIM ADVOCACY ORGANIZATIONS

Mothers Against Drunk Driving (MADD)
511 E. John Carpenter Fwy., #700
Irving, TX 75062
(214) 744-6233
Victim Hotline 1 (800) GET-MADD

National Assault Prevention Center
P.O. Box 02005
Columbus, OH 43202
(614) 291-2540

National Center for MISSING & EXPLOITED Children
2101 Wilson Blvd., Suite 550
Arlington, VA 22201-3053
(703) 235-3900

National Victim Center
2111 Wilson Blvd. Suite 300
Arlington, VA 22201
(703) 276-2880

National Crime Prevention Council
1700 K Street, NW, Suite 618
Washington, DC 20006
(202) 466-6272
(800) WE-PREVENT

National Institute for Mental Health
5600 Fishers Lane
Rockville, MD 20857
(301) 496-4000

NOVA (National Organization for Victim Assistance)
1757 Park Road, NW
Washington, D.C. 20010
(202) 232-6682

National Victim's Resource Center
P.O. Box 6000
Rockville, MD 20850
(800) 627-6872

Office for Victims of Crime
633 Indiana Ave., NW, Room 1342
Washington, DC 20024
(202) 307-0774

NATIONAL HEADQUARTERS OF SUPPORT ORGANIZATIONS

Children of Murdered Parents
P.O. Box 9317
Whittier, CA 90608
(310) 699-8427

Compassionate Friends
P.O. Box 3696
Oakbrook, IL 60522-3696
(708) 990-0010

Parents of Murdered Children
100 E. 8th St., B-41
Cincinnati, OH 45202
(513) 721-5683

The Arc
P.O. Box 300649
Arlington, TX 76010

National School Safety Center
4165 Thousand Oaks Blvd., Suite 290
Westlake Village, CA 91362
(805) 373-9977

Committee to Halt Useless College Killings (C.H.U.C.K.)
P.O. Box 188
Sayville, NY 11782
(516)567-1130

Security On Campus, Inc.
15 West Church Rd.
King of Prussia, PA 19406-3207
(215) 768-9330

NATIONAL MEDICAL RESOURCES

National Emergency Room Nurses Association
216 Higgin Rd
Partridge, IL 60068
(708) 698-9400

National Head Injury Foundation
333 Turnpike Rd.
Southborough, MA 01772

Spinal Cord Society
Rt. 5, Box 22a, Wendell Rd.
Fergus Falls, MN 56537
(214) 739-5252

Sunny Von Bulow Coma & Head Trama Foundation
555 Masison Ave. #32001
New York, NY 10023
(212) 753-5003

International Association for Healthcare Security & Safety
P.O. Box 637
Lombard, IL 60148
(708) 953-0990

GUN CONTROL

Handgun Control, Inc.
1225 Eye St. N.W., Room 1100
Washington, D.C. 20005
(202) 898-0792

Coalition To Stop Gun Violence
100 Maryland Ave., NE
Washington, D.C. 20002
(202) 544-7190

COURTS/SECURITY

International Association of Chiefs of Police
1110 N. Glebe, Suite 200
Arlington, VA 22201
(800) 843-4227

National Center for State Courts
300 Newport Avenue
Williamsburg, VA 23187-8798

National Sheriffs' Association
1450 Duke St.
Alexandria, VA 22314
(703) 836-7827

INDEX

ORDER FORM

Pathfinder Publishing of California
458 Dorothy Ave.
Ventura, CA 93003
Telephone (805) 642-9278   FAX (805) 650-3656

Please send me the following books from Pathfinder Publishing:

_____Copies of **Violence in our Schools, Hospitals and Public Places** @ $22.95 Hard Cover	$____
@ $14.95 Soft Cover	$____
_____Copies of **Violence in the Workplace** @ $22.95 Hard	$____
Violence in the Workplace @ $14.95 Soft	$____
_____Copies of **Beyond Sympathy** @ $9.95	$____
_____Copies of **Final Celebrations** @ $9.95	$____
_____Copies of **Living Creatively With Chronic Illness** @ $11.95	$____
_____Copies of **No Time For Goodbyes** @ $9.95	$____
_____Copies of **Stop Justice Abuse** @ $8.95	$____

Sub-Total	$____
Californians: Please add 7.25% tax.	$____
Shipping*	$____
Grand Total	$____

I understand that I may return the book for a full refund if not satisfied.

Name:_____

Address:_____
_____ZIP:_____

*SHIPPING CHARGES U.S.
Books: Enclose $2.50 for the first book and .50c for each additional book. UPS: Truck; $4.00 for first item, .50c for each additional. UPS Air: $7.50 for first item, $.75 for each additional item.